PRAISE WORKS!

PRAISE WORKS!

Merlin Carothers

Logos International
Plainfield, New Jersey

Preface

Not every prisoner is some criminal a judge has sentenced for a violation of the law of the State. Not every prison is made of stone and steel.

The hard, black, cold bars of insane asylums surround some of the blackest prisons in the world. They are like solid granite mountains, immovable and permanent. Millions of people are locked up, and many are tied down, in these monuments of man's failure to find the solution for mental agony.

Millions of others — you may be one of them — are not locked up in an actual physical building, but are imprisoned just as surely in prisons of their own making. They are so fettered by their fears and frustrations, their problems and angers, their unforgiveness and unbelief, that they cannot enjoy the liberty Christ died to give them, nor the abundant life He promised to those who would take hold of it by faith.

But there is relief. There is a way out of even the darkest prisons of despair and self-pity. Miracles are happening today. I could tell you of thousands, but I must limit this book to only a few real, live illustrations of what God is doing in people who are alive today.

Prisons of all kinds are being invaded with praise. Your prison, whatever its form, can be invaded, and you can be transformed by a joy that passes your understanding. Learn the secret of *freedom through praise* and you will see your situation change. Better yet, you yourself will be changed, never to be a prisoner again. Freedom is real. Freedom is forever. Freedom comes through praise.

Stand fast therefore in the liberty wherewith Christ hath made us free, and be not entangled again with the yoke of bondage. (Gal. 5:1)

Hey, God!

Frank Foglio, author of *Hey, God!* and an International Director of the Full Gospel Business Men, told me one of the most remarkable accounts of freedom through praise I have ever heard. He wanted me to share it with you.

Frank's daughter was injured in an automobile accident. Her brain was severely damaged, and although many thousands of prayers were made for her recovery, her condition grew steadily worse. Finally, she had to be placed in the "hopeless" ward of an institution for the mentally ill. It was the very end of the line.

Patients in the ward were so far removed from reality that their families seldom came to visit them. One patient had been strapped down for twelve years because of violence. Other inmates sat passive, staring at nothing, their vacant eyes reflecting brains emptied of all knowing. Still others lay rigid in beds, without sight or motion. Vegetables. Frank's daughter had clawed her way out of straitjackets and tried to hang herself with a bed sheet.

It had been seven years since the accident, and the absolute hopelessness of the situation began to take its toll of a very tough Italian. Frank's faith in God started to waver.

On one very difficult journey to the institution, Frank was arguing with God.

"How could You be a God of love? I wouldn't permit such a thing to happen to my daughter if I had the power to prevent it. You could heal her. But You won't. Don't You love people as much as even I do? You must not." Frank felt his anger rising against God.

"Praise Me," a Voice said to him.

"What for?" Frank replied.

"Praise Me that your daughter is where she is."

"Never!" he spit out. "I would rather die than do that." God had no right to ask him to praise Him when God wasn't

1

doing His own job of showing His love for people.

Frank remembered hearing a tape about giving thanks in everything. He had been deeply moved by the message, but at that moment he was in no mood to put it into practice.

"Thank Me that your daughter is exactly where she is," the Voice said again.

"God, I couldn't praise You if I tried. And I'm not going to try, because I don't believe I should."

As Frank continued toward the mental home, the Holy Spirit worked in his heart, and he felt his attitude begin to soften. He said, "Well, God, I would praise You if I could — but I just can't."

A little further along, he confessed, "I would praise You, but You would have to help me."

After arriving at the institution, Frank went through the necessary procedures to get clearance to get into the most restricted part of one of the buildings. It always took a long while to get into his daughter's ward. Sometimes, he wondered why he continued to come. His daughter didn't recognize him. She didn't know him from a stone on the ground.

Finally, Frank was in the last waiting room, the one that separated him from the ward. One steel door remained to be opened. Standing before it, Frank Foglio heard the calm and firm voice of God one more time:

"Thank Me that your daughter is exactly where she is."

The disobedience, the unwillingness, the hardness of heart had melted away. The stony heart of anger and bitterness and unfaith had somehow been replaced by a responsive heart of flesh. Frank, his throat choked with emotion, whispered his surrender:

"Okay, God. I thank You that my daughter is where she is. I know that You love her more than I do."

At that moment a vaguely familiar voice cried out, "I want my daddy, I want my daddy."

The attendant opened the door, and Frank raced to his daughter's compartment. Clothed in her right mind, she threw out her arms and embraced her father. Nurses, attendants, and guards gathered around to weep their joy.

Frank says, "Tell everyone our daughter is home now with us. We *know* that God always wants us to praise Him, regardless of how things look."

My Comments

It took Frank only a few minutes to tell his story, and it took only a few minutes for you to read it. But try to picture the seven long years of anxiety, frustration, tears, and fearful prayers. God saw their need, from the very beginning, and longed to supply it, but He had to wait patiently — to let them learn what they needed to know.

One day Frank walked with his daughter to the platform of our new church in Escondido, California. Her shining face and happy laughter were a testament of joy to the congregation. The Holy Spirit of God caused praise to rise within me:

"Oh, thank You, God, for teaching me the freedom You have provided through praise. Help me to share this glorious good news with the whole world."

You may be laboring over your own problem and be nearly ready to give up. How long have you been struggling to find an answer? How great has your pain been? God has a perfect solution to your problem. He will bring heaven on earth to you at the right time, and in the right way. Praise Him, trust Him, believe in Him. Freedom is yours!

Happy is the man whom God correcteth: therefore despise not thou the chastening of the Almighty: For he maketh sore, and bindeth up: he woundeth, and his hands make whole. He shall deliver thee in six troubles; yea, in seven there shall no evil touch thee. (Job 5:17-19)

From an Attorney

Dear Brother in Christ,

Fourteen years ago at age forty-two I was the D.A. of our county and a practicing alcoholic. I still had my wife, although our marriage was shot. My wife says that the only reason that we stayed together was that one or both of us were always too drunk to pack. In trying to find some answers for myself, I had purchased a Revised Standard Version of the Bible and a *Halley's Bible Handbook*. I used to sit down with the Bible, the reference book, and a fifth of whiskey, and when the whiskey was gone, I would curse because the Bible held no answers for me. About this time I was getting up to attend an early Bible study breakfast held at a restaurant. I usually showed up very belligerent, with a terrific hangover. Surprisingly enough, the men attending never threw me out, although they must have wanted to.

I started praying to whatever power caused the earth to turn, the tides to come and go, the rain to fall, that He would help me for one day not to take a drink. Somewhere along the line, I came to believe that He was helping me, and after a few months, I made a decision for Christ. I was so overjoyed with what the Lord was doing for me that I tried to share with church people. Most of them looked at me like I was crazy. Because I just couldn't keep quiet, I started sharing with prisoners in the jail and giving out modern translations of the New Testament to prisoners who would take them. The Holy Spirit converted many of these prisoners.

Because I was so nervous during my first year of sobriety, I used to ask God every day to make me less nervous. After a year of sobriety, I was in Portland having dinner at an AA club, and I mentioned that despite my prayers, I was more nervous after a year's sobriety than I had been before. One of the girls said, "Don't worry about it. Many of the members in Portland had the same thing. They called it 'Frantic serenity.'"

4

I had to laugh at myself, and later the thought came to me that maybe I'd been going about this thing the wrong way. I remembered how during the war and at other times when I had used up every bit of physical strength, I had always been able to draw on my nervous energy and keep going when the other men could not. So I decided that maybe being nervous was a gift from God, and I should be thanking Him instead of demanding that He relieve me.

So I started thanking God every day for being so nervous — and that is when a miracle took place. I became calm with my nervousness. I am sure that I am the same individual as always, but since I thank God, I am no longer fighting against nervousness, and therefore it no longer bugs me. For years, Paul had been telling me in his letters to thank God in all circumstances. Off and on I remembered to do it, but this summer when we acquired your two books, *Prison to Praise* and *Power in Praise*, it was brought home to me again.

About a month ago, I had an absolutely disastrous week in court, losing three cases in a row. I was able to say, "Lord, I can't see how this can possibly work out for good for my clients, but thank You anyway." Surprisingly enough, I am beginning to see that it is working out for my clients' own good, as I'm sure that it always does in my life, in making me more and more dependent on the Lord instead of upon myself.

My Comments

Lawyers, doctors, and specialists in many fields are stepping forward to say, "It works." Unbelievers are being forced to take another look at God's promises. The reactions are varied, but in some way they are all saying, "It sounds absolutely crazy, but praising God for everything turns a rotten life into a fresh new experience."

I Wouldn't Believe It

A friend of mine sent me a copy of *Prison to Praise.* I read and enjoyed it, but I went around warning people they had better be careful, as it could be taken wrong. Although I thought I *understood* it, I could not bring myself to thank God for something He did not cause. I know sickness, sorrow, and pain are from the enemy.

Two years passed, and I began to have all kinds of symptoms of a physical ailment. I put up with the pain for six months. Then I went to the physician and found that I had gall bladder trouble. I told the Lord I was going to try praising Him and not complain anymore to my husband or anyone.

This was on Monday. The next day, your book *Power in Praise* was given to me. I started reading it and could hardly put it down, but at the same time I kept saying to myself, "I will not say it, I will not say it." I cried at some incident in each chapter. I could tell the Holy Spirit was all over me and all over the book. Finally I said, "Thank You, Lord, for my gall bladder," and He said, "What kind of gall bladder?" I began to cry all the more and had to quit reading as I could not see. Later I returned to the book after doing some housework and read where a couple had thanked God for their totally psychotic daughter! I thought, "If they can thank God for her being completely insane, I can surely muster up enough courage to thank Him for my bad gall bladder." It did take a lot of something I didn't know I had, but still weeping, I managed to cry out, "Thank You, Lord, for my rotten gall bladder."

Instantly, the pain began to leave. I discovered I had been rebelling against God, for I was rebelling against the Truth of His Word, which is Jesus. I thank the Lord for this "new" concept that is 2,000 years old. I knew it was right and that you were quoting the Word of God, but in my rebellion, I had refused to see it. How I praise God that He has opened my eyes.

My Comments

There are many things which we refuse to see in God's Word. We often decide what we want to believe and cling to that regardless of what we see. Another person could be overflowing with joy and have many evidences of the power of God working in his life, but if his life does not measure up to our own interpretation of the Bible, we could refuse to see what God is doing. God has promised to bless and use anyone who will trust Him. Are you willing to believe that He can bless even you?

Word of Mouth

I shall never be able to thank God enough for allowing me to sit in on three of your services. Your message on praising God has changed my whole life, even though I had been a Spirit-filled Christian for nearly thirty-five years. Since hearing you and letting the message of praising God for all things really take deep root in me, I've been able to victoriously overcome battles I've had for nearly thirty years of marriage. I'll never cease to tell others about it, and I have already seen others miraculously delivered.

My Comments

Reading about praising God does help us, but hearing about it from others can have an even greater effect. You can let the praise of your lips influence the lives of those around you. You will perhaps be amazed at the hundreds of opportunities you can find every day to say, "Thank You, Lord," for all the little things that happen. Your praise will be contagious to others. They will pass it on to others. Your casual, yet intentional praise, will spread around the world.

I Was a Wreck

Dear Chaplain Carothers,

It is 2:30 A.M., and I have just finished reading *Power in Praise.* I will start my testimony where it all began.

My parents divorced in 1951 when I was three years of age. All of my growing-up years were spent in misery. I grew up an emotional cripple, with a lovely facade to hide it all. In desperation and loneliness, I married a boy I did not love, could not love, because I was a homosexual. The marriage ended in divorce, of course, but only after I had borne a child. I gladly received custody of our son and went to work to supplement the child support I received.

These events brought me up to this time last year. I was fairly content, financially secure, and had no need, or desire for God. To fill the void where God belonged in my life, I blew pot and involved myself with a boy many years my junior. I went my way for the biggest part of the summer, then in late July I took LSD, and my life turned a corner. I had a bad, horrifying trip, and when I sought help to come down from it, I was rejected by my family. Because of that bad trip, I lost my job and spent the month of January in a mental institution. Since that day, almost a year ago, my "bad luck" has continually increased.

Last January I was baptized in the Holy Spirit and delivered from homosexuality. I was happy and thankful, momentarily. Then I turned from God, and my worldly problems overwhelmed me again. Bills and trouble have piled up in irritating stacks. I have no job, no prospects, and no money, and an old car.

Only a few hours ago, I was in a charismatic prayer meeting and was given your book. I didn't feel any better for having gone to the meeting, but when I started your book, the changes began. I read a few pages and cried and read some more and cried some more. The clarification was almost instant. Now I know why I'm in such a mess. Rebellious as I

8

have been, God had to break me to get me back to Him. Praise God! I tearfully begged His forgiveness and thanked Him for the circumstances that brought me back. I know now that my life will be changed forever more. I really understand that Jesus died for me. Your book was the key. There aren't words to describe my joy.

That the trial of your faith, being much more precious than of gold that perisheth, though it be tried with fire, might be found unto praise and honour and glory at the appearance of Jesus Christ: Whom having not seen, ye love; in whom, though now you see him not, yet believing, ye rejoice with joy unspeakable and full of glory. (I Pet. 1:7-8)

My Comments

What a beautiful testimony of the love of God persisting in reaching down to redeem the lost. This person is able to see the love of God now that the past is behind her. Frequently people get hung up on the present, and cannot see what God is doing, or permitting to happen. Please learn from this letter and apply it in your own life, and in the lives of those you love. Instead of being filled with fear and impatience, believe that God is working for their good. God will take whatever Satan is doing to your loved ones, and use it to bend their will and draw them to Christ. God will not force their obedience, but He will bend them and do whatever He can to bring them to a right choice. Do not fight against God by being filled with fear that He is in no way involved with the conflict people are in. God can and will use your faith to bless those who are in need.

P.S. It has been several months since this woman entered into a life of praise. She says her joy and strength are continually increasing.

He Needed Help

Dear Pastor Carothers,

A man in our office was in trouble, but he didn't know it. He was very well educated, thought he knew more than the boss did, and frequently made his attitude known to the boss himself. It was very evident to me that the boss was getting more and more disgusted with this man. If he were to be fired, I knew the man would probably fall apart. He had more problems than anyone I've ever known. His wife had divorced him and taken nearly everything he had. He was a sexual deviate; his nerves were so bad his hands would shake when he was perturbed about anything; his stomach was upset all the time; he was an alcoholic; and — I could go on and on.

I felt very sorry for this man, and I prayed for him daily, but he continued to get worse. He was demoted to a very inferior position, but had no understanding that it was his own fault. Your book, *Prison to Praise,* was given to me, and I decided to try praising God for this man. I thanked God for the man as he was, and I believed God would use his problems to help him. At this time, I heard the Lord speak to me as I had never heard Him before! He said, "Go to his church, and pray for him."

"But Lord," I protested, "he is Catholic, and I am Protestant."

"Go to his church and pray."

So, to his church I went. It was the United Nations Catholic Chapel in New York. Everything was very strange to me, but while praying, I experienced a wonderful joy and peace that God was going to help that man. God must have really lit my face up, for the priest sent someone to ask who I was.

When I returned to the office, to my amazement I heard the man saying to the boss, "I'm sorry, sir. I made a mistake." He had never shown any humility in the office before. From that day on, his attitude and conduct continued to change for the better. I'm excited about the idea of praising the Lord for people as they are.

My Comments

We are surrounded with people having every problem we can think of. Our natural reaction is to avoid those who have the greatest needs. They are obnoxious, arrogant, weak, or act as if they do not want our help. But if they come to our attention, God has a specific reason for bringing them into our lives. Seeing that they need help takes no love on our part. If we learn to thank the Lord for them as they are, He will release His love in us that He can use to help them. Please do not turn away from those you dislike. They are God's gift to you. They will help your own need to learn about Christ's love. When you recognize the feeling of agitation rising in you, let the power of praise counteract it, and Jesus will use your praise to meet their need, and besides this, your own distress will be turned to joy as you see God working.

Whenever someone gives himself over to rejoicing and thanking God for all things, a remarkable thing begins to happen. Other gifts of the Spirit begin to be manifested in that person in a beautiful way. Praise for and to God literally opens the way for the Holy Spirit to bring new insight and understanding in many ways. In the above case, the writer was given a spiritual insight which enabled her to know about material things. More and more people are being given wisdom they never had as they praise and thank God. This is the spiritual kind of supernatural knowledge and wisdom that has the anointing of God. It is this kind of perception that the devil tries to imitate when people search for knowledge of unknown things to increase their own ego. Knowledge received through the Holy Spirit by faith in Christ need never be feared or shunned. All of the gifts of the Holy Spirit are good and are to be used for the glory of God.

Every good gift and every perfect gift is from above, and cometh down from the Father of lights. (James 1:17)

Deliberate Sin

Dear Sir,

This is the first time that I have really ever thought about praising God for all things and for every situation. I am still puzzled by one thing: Should we praise Him for sin in our lives? If I, through a rebellious or negligent heart, sin, I have gone against God's plan for my life, haven't I? He didn't want me to sin, did He?

For example, I know I should be meeting with the Lord every day in His Book and in prayer. That requires discipline on my part. But if I, because I don't feel like it, decide not to have my quiet time that day, I am sinning. So, how can I praise God for not having my quiet time? I know He wanted me to have one. He's commanded that we meditate on His Word that it might become part of us. If I deliberately neglect to do what He has commanded, shouldn't I be asking God for forgiveness? Maybe what I'm saying is that praising God implies that it wasn't my fault, that He wanted it to happen to me. But does God want sin in our lives? He abhors it, does He not? It hurts Him, doesn't it?

Another example, an extreme one: If I deliberately plotted to kill someone, went out and did it, how could I praise God for that?

I can see praising God for the fact that my car konks out, but can I really praise Him if it konked out because I deliberately refused to put gas in it?

Really, I am confused. Is there anything you can say that would answer some of these questions?

There is one area in my life where Satan continually bugs me and that's my immoral past. I'm now twenty-one, and am attending a university. God moved in my life in a great way about two and one-half years ago and I committed my life to Him as best as I knew how. Up until that time, I had not been the purest of women. But I want to forget that. I know that God has forgiven me for those things, but Satan keeps bringing these experiences into my mind. It says in Colossians

3 and Philippians 4 (and a lot of other places) that we should set our mind on godly things. I try to do this. But I must admit that Satan sometimes wins.

Tying in with my whole icky past is the whole thing about masturbation. This causes a great deal of sorrow in my life. I know it hurts Jesus, but the temptation is so strong sometimes, that I just put Him out of my mind. Afterwards, I'm just *so* grieved. *"Why* did I do that?" I ask myself.

I'm praying really hard about these two things — my past that I want to have wiped out of my mind, and masturbation.

If you have time when you finish reading this letter, I would really appreciate it and thank the Lord if you would pray with me that Christ will have victory over Satan in these areas of my life. I don't want to sin.

My Answer

I know that it sounds really strange to praise God for sin in our lives. But if you fail to praise God for this one thing, you open wide the door to fail to praise Him for many things.

If you determine in your heart that you will praise Him for all things, a major victory has been won.

It is true that you may have to suffer in this life for the sin that you commit. But there is another glorious reality about sin. It points you to your urgent need of Christ's forgiveness. The more you believe He forgives you, the more you do not want to sin. Often the less we believe He forgives us, the more inclined we are to proceed in our old sinful nature.

The attitude you have taken toward God regarding devotions is simply an overflow from your lack of understanding of His great love for you, just as you are. Devotions should not be an act of obedience to God. Devotions are an opportunity to hear from a God who loves us, and to talk to Him. Until you really understand this, devotions will never be a real part of your life. Two human beings could never share a real love relationship while thinking they would be guilty of sin if they did not read the letters written to one another. They might say, "I have

13

sinned against you because I failed to read the letter you wrote to me," or "I failed to write to you, therefore I sinned." God does not want our obligation; He wants our love.

If you were deliberately plotting to kill someone, I seriously doubt if you would be praising God while you were doing it. If following the act you then realized your sin and asked for God's forgiveness, I believe He could very well use your sin to work out something good, just as he used the sin of killing His own Son to bring salvation to mankind.

All of the elements in your letter indicate that you are bound by an inward fear that you are continually breaking God's laws and are therefore unworthy of His love, or of the right to praise Him for everything. The more you praise God for your weaknesses or failures, the less you will want to do these things. Is it not clear to you that your present method of feeling guilty has not helped you? Why don't you try the scriptural method of praising God every time you do something you know to be wrong? Your praise and thanksgiving will remind you of His love for you, and will definitely lift you into a higher spiritual plane. Satan, who tempts you, cannot stand an atmosphere of worship and praise to God. Anytime we do something that is weak and then turn to praise and thanking God for our weakness, a marvelous power is released to help us receive Christ's strength in place of our own weakness. To understand that God loves you just as you are is one of the greatest needs you will ever have as a human being. Your physical acts, whatever they may be, are never as likely to separate you from God as will your lack of love for Him. Therefore I say, "Praise God for everything."

My Comments

Never use praise as an excuse for sin. Use sin as a reason for praise. Our praise to God, for whatever reason, brings a stronger realization of His presence and with it a desire to repent and be transformed by His love.

Sick, Sick, Sick

Dear Merlin Carothers,

A remark you made in *Answers to Praise* prompts me to write. You said, "If the kind of praying you have been used to has left you with nothing but discouragement, try the prayer of praise and thanksgiving."

I don't want this to be a completely negative letter, but I have to tell it like it is. I am going through a terrible time. I see my personality and character disintegrating. Despair and worry are killing me.

My daughter has an affliction that does not allow her to grow or develop as a young girl should. She is only four feet seven and is almost seventeen years old. She is lonely, feels rejected, and is emotionally disturbed. She doesn't have a single friend to go out with. She is home alone seven nights and days a week. Surely this is not a loving God's plan for her. She has to take hormones for the rest of her life, and we know hormones are dangerous.

Now, how do I pray? Do I thank God for her affliction, for her loneliness, for her unhappiness? Do I thank God for her misery and complete lack of the normal fun and companionship she so longs for? Please, please, how do I pray, what do I say? Our Lord Jesus did not like to see illness and unhappiness, and He healed.

Please help me out of this web of confusion and hopelessness. There is so much in the way. My relationship with my husband is empty, and always I'm dogged by feelings of guilt. Even when I am humanly justified, I feel guilty. That's fine if the Holy Spirit is convicting me, but along with conviction I need help.

I really don't know how to pray anymore. I love Jesus, but I am far from Him. I know only God can help me and my family. Can you tell me what is wrong? Something is holding me back, but what? Please, if you can, tell me what I need to do and how to pray and I'll do it.

My Answer

Jesus hung on the cross alone, betrayed, denied and hated. He suffered an agony of body and soul that few humans could understand. But what does that do for you? His suffering was to provide you and your family health, strength, and happiness. He wants you to take hold of them. Believe that He is using your problems to help you, and let your faith in Jesus begin to grow.

You have the right to think about whatever you want to think about. Up to this point, you have chosen to think about everything bad. Choose now to praise God for His love and the gift of His Son seventy times seven times every day. Every time a fearful or unhappy thought comes, reject it, and thank Him for sight, hearing, limbs, lungs — everything you can think of. Healing will begin to work in you. What had been a sad, unlovely disposition will begin to shine.

Friends will notice. Your husband will. Nothing is so beautiful as a woman filled with praise to God. Your praise will bring healing to your entire family! Thousands of families with equal or worse problems have found complete and total healing. You are not one bit different from them.

I am believing with you now *for healing*. Believe with me. Your testimony will then reach many others.

My Comments

I know that when your leg hurts, it always hurts you more than it does me, even if my leg is injured ten times worse. Your pain is felt by *you*. But remember this, your pain is felt by God, too. He understands and wants to heal you. He is limited only by your faith to believe Him!

Jesus . . . healed them all. (Matt. 12:15)

16

Cancer and Leukemia

Dear Chaplain Carothers,

I have read your book, *Prison to Praise*, and I can't resist writing to let you know how much it has helped me. When I was ten years old, my father killed my mother. He was sent to prison, and I to live with an aunt and uncle. I married when I was twenty, and at twenty-two I lost my husband to cancer, but I was blessed with his child. Now, six years later, my present husband and I have been told that our daughter has leukemia. The news was shattering to me. I didn't see how I could face two bouts with that dreaded disease.

My first urge was to race home and kill myself, but before I got home, my plan left my mind. I returned to the hospital with an overpowering urge to talk to our preacher. He came at once and offered us his help. That night at church I went down front asking for special prayer. During the prayer session, I forgave my father for killing my mother and prayed that he could receive peace of mind.

I have been praying for our daughter's total recovery, but until I read your book, I was not praising God for these trials. I've now got a new understanding of God and His will. Thank you for sharing your experiences.

My Comments

If we try to carry the burdens of "tragedies" in our families, we will often be given the suggestion by Satan, "Go ahead and kill yourself." If we turn these problems over to God, His Spirit will suggest, "Be at peace. I will abundantly supply everything that is needed." The sick often say, "But where was God when I needed Him most?" He was right there urging you to give your problem to Him. If you had praised Him, your faith would have released His power to supply perfect peace within the very center of your being. This letter illustrates the release from fear and anger that God wants to give every human being. The problem itself may remain, but the end result is completely changed.

17

Grin and Bear It

Dear Mr. Carothers,

I will start by telling you that I heard you speak in St. Louis in August of 1970 at a Full Gospel Businessmen's convention. When you began speaking, I sort of gritted my teeth, as I had a preconceived idea of what a message by an Army Colonel would be like. I settled back in my seat, prepared to grin and bear it, not too happy about the whole matter. Then, much to my surprise, you really caught my interest. Your message was quite long, but not nearly long enough to suit me. I wanted you to go on for hours. Needless to say, my preconceived ideas were tossed out the window, and as I have told many people since, your message left a greater impression on me than any I had ever heard before, and I had heard thousands.

I bought your book, *Prison to Praise,* and read it over and over. It really changed my life. I began praising God for everything in my life, both good and bad, and it really increased my joy and peace. It's so much better to be happy and thankful than unhappy and complaining.

My Comments

Yes, being thankful for everything is very difficult for the average person to grasp, and so is atomic energy. Yet most people believe in atomic power, because they have heard about it from sources they consider reliable. Reliable sources in the form now of at least a million people in our own country, and thousands in other countries, are declaring that praising God for everything is powerfully setting them free from pain they had struggled with for many years. My suggestion is, "If it works, why not use it?"

If this counsel or this work be of men, it will come to nought: But if it be of God, ye cannot overthrow it. (Acts 5:38-39)

18

Electric Polisher

Dear Sir,

I have postponed writing this letter for over a month for two reasons: (1) I wanted to make sure that the spectacular change that has taken place in my life as a result of following your advice to praise God in everything was not just a fluke or one of those "highs" that happen in the Christian life from time to time; (2) Once thoroughly convinced that this was not a passing thing, I haven't been able to think of words in which I could adequately express my appreciation to you for yielding yourself to God so that He could use you to tell us these truths.

I could go on for forty pages, but I'll spare you that. I would like, however, to tell you of one incident that happened. About four or five days after I began to take seriously this business of praising God in everything, I was working at my business, polishing and waxing cars for dealers and getting them ready for sale, when the buffer or electric polisher I was using snatched the heavy chrome strip off the side of a car and wound it up around the "wheel" of the buffer like a clockspring while the end of the strip slapped my right wrist as 2800 RPM. I couldn't shut the buffer off because the switch was defective, and I couldn't drop it. I had to go and pull the plug.

I suppose the end of the strip struck my wrist 400 or 500 times. It was *very* painful! But do you know what I was astounded to find myself saying while this was going on? "Praise the Lord, Thank You, Jesus," over and over again. I wouldn't have expected to find myself cursing, but I would no more have expected to find myself praising God under those circumstances than to be dancing a jig on top of a new car.

I was sure my wrist was ruined. I was particularly concerned because my left wrist has been "frozen," made entirely immobile by osteomyelitis, ever since I was thirteen.

While one stiff wrist has never been any great handicap to me, the possibility of having two of them was not attractive.

Later, I was taken in my right wrist with the worst pain I've ever experienced. It lasted about two minutes, although it seemed like half an hour, and again I found myself saying, "Thank You, Jesus," over and over again. My speaking could not have been more "involitional" (if I know what that means). It just came out of me. I believe that in that moment God set and healed the bones that were broken in my wrist.

When the doctor x-rayed my wrist, she asked me if I had ever injured that wrist before. I told her that I hadn't, and she said, "That's very strange." There was evidence in the Xrays that some of the bones had been broken and healed.

I have other problems in my life, but there is evidence that God is working in them, and I know that they are as good as done. I am thanking God for the solutions and enjoying being relieved of the problems. I don't know how He's going to work them out, but I know He will. Isn't He a wonder!

I am looking forward to thanking you in person for the immeasurable help that your books have been to me in bringing me to see the truth about God's wonderful provision in these matters. If I don't see you while I am in residence in this rather dilapidated house in which I currently reside, I shall certainly search for you near the Throne, so that I may personally express my love and gratitude.

My Comments

There is nothing complicated about simple faith in God. It only seems complicated because we, in our frustrations, make it so. Childlike faith is nothing more than believing God has supplied our need even before we see any evidence that He has done so.

20

I Don't Understand

Dear Sir,

A friend gave me *Power in Praise* and *Prison to Praise.* I read every word. I have been expecting something to happen to me, too. I pray and pray, and ask God to stop me from crying every day and feeling sorry for myself, but nothing happens.

My husband divorced me after nineteen years of marriage. He was not much fun, but he was very good to me. We were together all the time, and now I am alone, sixty-one years old, and so lonely and miserable. I cry every day, and it does not help one bit.

I don't understand why so many good things happen to those people in your book and nothing good happens to me. What can I do? I still love my husband and can't get him out of my mind. The few friends I have left are tired of my crying. So am I.

Could you please tell me what I can do? I have faith in the Lord, read the Bible every day, and go to church regularly.

My Answer

Yes, I would be glad to give you what advice I can. In your letter you write, "I have been expecting something to happen to me, too." In this sentence lies the answer to all of the other questions you have asked. If you were expecting something good to happen to you, you would be completely free of the other unpleasant things. *Expecting* God to do something brings faith, hope, and real joy. *Not expecting* brings fear, anxiety, and worry.

With this fear in your heart, it is a natural result that you cry all the time and find sadness does not help at all. You say that you don't understand why nothing good happens to you. What can you do? My answer is, start expecting good things from God. Start believing that He is using every

21

experience in your life to bring something good to you. Your faith will release all of God's power to do for you what He wants. Your own fear is the very thing that holds back His power.

You say, "I have faith in the Lord." This is exactly what I want you to have but what you do not have. I join you now in believing that God is going to use all of your experiences to bring you into His joy. Later, I will share with others what He has done for you.

We triumph even in our troubles, knowing that trouble produces endurance, endurance produces character, character produces hope, a hope which never disappoints us, since God's love floods our hearts through the Holy Spirit which has been given to us. (Rom. 5:3-5 Moffatt)

Discouraged Nun

Dear Mr. Carothers,

Praise be to God for your book, *Prison to Praise.* Until I read it, I was a discouraged Catholic nun. I was seriously thinking of giving up this life and God. But now, praising God for everything, I am sublimely happy and content in doing the work of the Lord in this life. The joy and peace I feel is something I had never felt before. I am getting my pupils to praise God for everything, also. If I could afford it, I would buy copies of your book and spread them around among all my discouraged friends.

Thanks again for making my life beautiful. God bless you always.

My Comments

You can find discouraged people in every walk of life. But God is using praise to bring deliverance everywhere.

22

From Prison

Dear Merlin,

I wanted to write you about how my life was revolutionized through praising the Lord for every difficult circumstance. I am in the county jail on a ten-year probation violation and on a burglary charge. I also have a narcotics charge pending against me, but my worries, grudges, strains, and fears have disappeared through God's gift of praise.

When I first came to the county jail, I was sick, and I mean sick with life. I was here two weeks when I read your book, *Prison to Praise.* That same day I accepted Jesus Christ as my Savior and Lord, and received the wonderful Baptism in the Holy Spirit. Then, a month later, I read *Power in Praise,* and that did it. Now my cell is filled with praise.

After reading *Prison to Praise* I was still a little confused about the power in praise, but when I read *Power in Praise,* my confusion disappeared. Life is so much more beautiful in this world now that I have the Heavenly Father and Son with me at all times. The Lord has showed me that being confined in a reformatory two times before was also part of His plan for me. I would appreciate it very much if you would pray with us for the Lord's lost sheep who are in our tank here at the jail. Pray that they will have the courage to lay down their lives for Jesus Christ.

My Comments

If God can turn a jail cell into a place of praise and joy, how about the place where *you* live? Would you like to do something for the inmates of the more than two million jail cells in the United States by providing copies of *Prison to Praise?* The Foundation of Praise has been established to help you do exactly that. During 1972, thirty-five men were murdered in the prisons of one state alone. How the power of God's Holy Spirit to change lives is needed in those places!

23

Son on Fire

Dear Colonel Carothers,

I read your book on praise and thought, "I could never praise God for my son being like he is. His dirty long hair, dirty clothes, such laziness he won't get a job, drunkenness and dope are too much for any mother to stand, let alone to be thankful for." But a nagging thought kept churning in my mind: "Nothing else has worked; maybe God is trying to tell me something."

One night, some of my son's friends brought him home and carried him into our living room. They laid his unconscious, drunken body on the hearth in front of the fireplace. When they left, I sat down in a chair and looked at him.

"God, how could I thank You for that?"

I heard, "I want you to thank Me."

"But I can't," was all I could say.

Suddenly, as I sat there looking at him, and shaking my head in despair, I saw smoke rising from my son! The flames in the fireplace had caught his clothes on fire! I ran over and smothered the blaze with my hands. While my hands were still on him, I had an overpowering urge to pray.

"Okay, God. I thank You for this my son exactly as he is." I couldn't help but weep as I prayed. To my surprise, my son sat straight up and said, "Mother, did you mean that?"

"Yes, I did son."

He went off to bed. The next morning I saw him in the bathroom with a big pair of scissors, cutting off his dirty hair. "Why are you doing that?" I asked him.

"I'm going to try to get a job, and I know I can't get one unless I cut some of this off." What a surprise that was! In the afternoon, he came back and said, "I haven't found a job yet, but I remembered something I want to do." He went into his bedroom and brought out two handfuls of materials he said were used for taking dope. "I don't know if I can change, mother, but I have a strong urge to try to be what you want me to be."

My Comments

God can do in a second what parents could not do in years of criticism, complaints, or urging. Parents may want many things from their children, but only God can change a human being. He can take everything — even the bad — and use it to help those we love. He may not always do it in the twinkling of an eye, but He has His own perfect time schedule.

The Wrath of God

Dear Sir,

I need your help. The church I have attended has taught me nothing but the wrath of God. This has put me in great bondage and fear. I seem to have no confidence in myself and no love for God. When I was younger, I loved God, but hearing about His wrath for so long has caused all love to leave me. It is difficult for me to explain how I can believe in God and yet not love Him. I know from what Jesus said that the most important thing is for me to love Him. What can I do if I don't love Him? Should I praise God that I don't love Him, or what should I praise Him for? I think of God as standing ready to punish me if I make a mistake. This is what I have been taught in the Word of God. Please pray for me and give me any help that you can.

My Answer

Many people have been helped by hearing about the wrath of God and have turned their lives to follow Him. However, it is true that many more have heard so much about God's wrath and so little about His love that their spirit has been wounded. You have apparently been wounded. I urge you to keep listening to the voice of the Holy Spirit as He tells you over and over, "God loves you just as you are." If you have accepted Christ as your Savior, you are now God's child. Of course, He may discipline you when you are disobedient, but this does not change your relationship. You are still His child. He loves you, and more than anything else, He wants you to love Him.

I will be in prayer with you that your love for God will grow steadily day by day. You can help by finding others and telling them that God loves them. As you spread His love to others, the Holy Spirit will move in your own spirit and cause your realization of God's love to grow.

My Comments

Satan has used religious people to spread the fear of God since he knows that God wants our love more than anything else. It is extremely difficult for many people to confess to themselves that they fear God but do not love Him. Without love for God, your Christian experience is flat, empty, and you will often have the feeling that you are missing something very important. When you stop grumbling and start praising, you will find a new experience with Him!

Transformed

The following letter is so unusual that you may find it difficult to believe. You may be offended by the writer's frankness, but her life-style is typical of a great segment of our American society.

Chaplain Carothers,

I knew I needed God when I woke up in a mental ward with restraints on my arms and legs. I had tried to commit suicide.

I've never had any love except God's. I was adopted when I was three days old. My brother was adopted after our mother died.

26

I have been a sinner all my life. I am nineteen now. When I was thirteen, I had sex with my brother. I thank God I had a miscarriage, but the whole story came out, and everyone in our town knew about me. I've never been able to talk or write to anyone about this until now.

I got married when I was fifteen. I had open-heart surgery the same year. I had a baby at sixteen, and another at seventeen. My husband left after our second baby was born, and we've been separated since then.

I began hanging around with some hippies, and I started taking downers. I had an operation to keep me from getting pregnant again, and sex became a part of every day of the week, usually with someone different each time.

I felt like no one loved me, so I took a whole bottle of sleeping pills, and ended up in the mental ward. In the hospital, I began to feel that there were people who cared about me. A nurse gave me your book, *Prison to Praise*. While reading it, I cried so much that my pillow was soaking wet. It slowly became real to me that God loved me. It was tough to thank Him for my past life, but I did, and then He made me into a new person. What I used to be is not what I am now! I am thankful that whatever I was, God used it to show me that He loves me.

My Comment

The agony of guilt and shame is usually more damaging to the human frame than the act of sin itself. Self-torture drives many people to self-destruction. Regardless of how far from God anyone is, they are transformed when they believe God loves them just as they are. If He loves them, they have to accept themselves. What psychiatrists cannot do in hundreds of hours of therapy is done in the twinkling of an eye by one brief moment of earnest praise to God.

Please don't waste your time trying to convince people they are sinners. Nearly every down and out person I have ever known knows he is bad. What he doesn't know is that God loves him enough to give him a new life, a brand-new life that is free from all guilt. How can you feel guilt over something another person did? He took "upon Himself" your sin.

If any man be in Christ, he is a new creature. (II Cor. 5:17)

I Disagree

Dear Mr. Carothers,

I recently read both of your books. I found them most helpful and inspiring. However, I would take issue with a statement on the very first page of *Power in Praise* — "The condition is part of His wonderful plan." I don't believe for a minute God wants us to live a life of degradation. He gives us a free choice to seek His will and guidance or to lead our lives in our own selfish fashion. How can God be blamed if we choose our way? I know that at any particular time in our lives — if we allow Him entry into our hearts — He can and will direct us, bringing something wonderful out of any situation.

After finishing the book, I'm convinced this is your thinking, too, and that the wording is misleading. My brother-in-law at sixty years of age is a broken, unfulfilled, selfish man due to his choosing to drink alcoholic beverages. His health is very poor after years of punishment to his body. He never sought God's guidance, and yet when his habit finally caught up with him, he blamed God. I believe it was a natural result of his disobedience, and that he is still buck-passing as he has done all these years. To say that this was God's will for his life is unthinkable. He had so many talents, so much to give others.

I really am searching for a clear-cut understanding and would appreciate your comments.

Incidentally, my husband and I are praying regularly together now. Yes, and thanking God for all things — good and bad. We know that things hold good as long as God is directing our lives. So you see, I am not taking issue with all that you say, for it has opened up a whole new way of thinking, and I'm grateful beyond words. Life is sweeter, more relaxed, more meaningful with Him as the center of all things. Thank you so very much.

My Answer

Dear Friend,

Thank you very much for your letter. I agree with you that many times people go outside of God's plan for them. This is the reason that I emphasize that all things work together for good to them that love God. If we do not love God and are not seeking His will, most of the things in our lives could work against us and go against God's plan. However, I do know that God loves all men and even though they are fighting against Him and ruining their bodies, God is still exerting His influence to help them. Even acute alcoholism can be used by God to bring a person to accept Christ.

Let us release our faith to believe God is working even in the sad condition of your brother-in-law and is using his problem to draw him to Christ. God will certainly honor our faith and trust in Him. This does not mean that He approves or that we approve; it simply means we are trusting Him to use everything to help those whom He loves. The fact that many do not immediately respond to His love is not our concern. We may not understand, but we must trust that God is permitting whatever influences He knows could best help any man to realize his need. We must recognize that God's highest plan for your brother-in-law's life is that he come to know Christ as Savior.

We can now release our faith to God and believe that He is using even a wasted life to draw one person to Himself. Remember that Jesus came into the world to find that one lost sheep. He is concerned over the ninety-nine, but gave His life for the one who wasted his own life in riotous living. As God used the experiences of the prodigal son to bring him to his senses, God will also use the experiences of all men to draw them toward Himself. Those who do not respond must fight against the love of God and do so to their own destruction.

My Comments

All over the world there are living examples of wasted lives. Many are wasted because of evil governments and evil in the world, but I believe that God is using even all of these forces to draw to a completion His plan for the world. There are many things that I do not understand, but I do not question my Heavenly Father. Only He as God can understand what He is doing. I as the "created" am not going to argue with my Creator. He has given His own Son to give me eternal life. I accept that as His ultimate sacrifice in order that I might have life. I believe that in His plan there is the opportunity of eternal life for all men. This extends to every man who has ever lived. I do not profess to understand how this reaches out to those who have never heard the good news of the Gospel, but I believe that it does. How God operates this plan I leave in His own care.

That was the true light, which lighteth every man that cometh into the world. (John 1:9)

A Nurse Prays

Dear Reverend Carothers,

I won't bore you with my sinful story, but I will say this. Due to strife in my marriage, I began to seek God and pray and read my Bible. I still didn't feel any great release, even after the problems began to straighten out, but I continued to read and pray.

I am a nurse, and I do private duty. One day I was taken from one case and placed on another who was a Christian with terminal cancer. This wonderful Christian asked me one day if I had read *Prison to Praise*. I told her no, so she said she would have her family bring it for me to read. As the days and weeks passed, my patient grew weaker and weaker. Often she would lapse into a coma or be heavily sedated. Most of the time she didn't know I was there, but the book was left in the room and I started reading it.

Due to the severity of my patient's illness, the room was kept in darkness. The window shades were taped down and the door was kept closed. No one entered the room except her doctor and the private duty nurses. I had opened a crack between the shade and window about one inch for enough light to read by. The more I read, the more God dealt with my heart. Finally, I was led to get my Bible out of my pocketbook and fall on my knees to pray.

The Bible was a Testament my only son handed me the day he left home to attend college. He had been a Christian since he was twelve years old. With no help from me, he used to get up and go to Sunday school, leaving me asleep in bed. Other boys called him a square and a sissy because he carried his Bible in his car and tried to witness for Christ.

As I knelt with my Bible in my hands, suddenly the darkened room became as bright as if a powerful floodlight had been turned on. I turned around to see who had come into the room, but no one was there, and the door closed. But I had seen a great light, and I had felt my heart open to receive it.

I started reading your book again and this is what I read: "My son, what I wanted you to know was that you never again have to worry whether anyone will overcharge you, hurt you, or mistreat you, unless it is My will. Your life is in the palm of My hand, and you can trust Me for all things. As you continue to thank Me in all circumstances, you will see how perfectly I work out every detail of your life." At that moment I knew that Christ was my Savior.

All this happened about 1:00 P.M., and the patient had not aroused, moved, or spoken on my shift, but as I accepted Christ, she stirred and said, "Joyce, come hold my hand, and let's pray."

My son almost shouted when I telephoned and told him I had accepted Christ as my Savior. In his rejoicing, he said, "Mother, God has answered my prayers. I have been praying for you to become a Christian for many years."

I have bought many copies of *Prison to Praise* for different people, along with *Power in Praise* and *Answers to Praise*. I am praying that God will lead you to write more books. You have solved my Christmas shopping problem as I plan to give each one on my list your three books and a copy of the *Living Bible*. I only wish I had enough money to place a copy of *Prison to Praise* in every hospital room and jail cell in this town.

When people who have known me for many years tell me that I even have a different facial expression from the one I used to have, I tell them I am so happy to have Jesus for my friend that I want to shout it to the world. Praise the Lord!

My Comment

Many people are becoming known as "one of those with a silly grin." A life of continual peace in Christ is intended for every child of God. God's promises are not held back from those who have problems. His promises are especially designed for those who do have problems. If you have felt "left out," start saying, "Praise the Lord." Think praise to Him continually, and His Spirit will begin a new work in you.

Let the people praise thee, O God; let all the people praise thee. (Ps. 67:5)

A Chaplain Receives

Dear Merlin,

While I was in Vietnam, I was struck by the singular lack of power in my life. I believed in miracles. In fact, if it hadn't been for the healing power of God, I would have died as a child. I could always point to that. I preached on miracles and encouraged people to believe God for them, and God did answer some of our prayers in Vietnam in a miraculous way. But somehow, I couldn't reach the drug addicts who were sincere in wanting and desiring help. I would hear them ask Jesus to come into their hearts, but no revolution took place.

I prayed and read the Word faithfully. And then I read your book. It started me to praising God for some things, but questions of war and horrendous accidents among the men acted as a block. I didn't see how I could praise God for such things as that.

Then came the clincher. I got my orders assigning me to Fort Belvoir. I didn't want Fort Belvoir, Washington, D.C., or anywhere on the East Coast. I wanted Fort Lewis or Fort Ord on the West Coast. When I called my wife via overseas phone, she wept about the assignment. Always before, I had believed that God led me in each assignment. Therefore, I never bothered anyone when my orders came through. This time I thought I would make an exception and go to the chief's office with some excuse and ask for re-assignment. But on the way to Fort Belvoir and the Washington area from San Francisco, I said, "No. I will leave this in the hands of God and thank Him." The post chaplain assigned me to the Religious Education/Hospital slot. I didn t like that. Religious Education was no favorite of mine, and I related poorly to medical personnel. But I was stuck with it.

One Monday, a Spirit-baptized Episcopalian woman came into my office to talk. She telephoned me later that day to say that I was going to be baptized in the Spirit within seven days.

"Great," I thought, "I'm a candidate for anything God has for me. He can whip it on me anytime." The next Sunday night, a Spirit-baptized couple came to our youth meeting and many young people were filled with the Holy Spirit. I thought that was fine.

"Let's just go up to the altar and praise God for what He has already done," I suggested.

We all went forward, and I knelt and just simply held my arms upward and said, "God, here I am at Your disposal. Just use me any way You can." With that, two young people came up and said, "God has just showed us you are going to be baptized in the Holy Spirit. Do you mind if we lay hands on you and pray?"

"No. Go right ahead." They prayed, and I felt nothing. I thought, "Well, that's par for the course."

Then one of them said, "Let it out, let it out."

And I thought, "Let what out?"

"Let it go," they said.

Then I realized, "Well, if they want me to make funny sounds, I can do that for them." I did, and still felt nothing.

They all said, "Praise God. He's received."

I wasn't sure what I had received. When they wanted to sing in tongues, I said to myself, "No way. This isn't of God, for certainly I would have some emotional response to God." I doubted my experience for a week, then decided I would take what happened on faith.

In the middle of the week following the experience, the senior chaplain called me into his office and said, "You are relieved of your job. I do not want any Pentecostal influence around our young people."

Since that time, the things I see God doing through me simply amaze me. I marvel at His love and mercy.

My mother and father now speak in tongues. A neighbor lady was healed of epilepsy and baptized in the Spirit along with four others. Fifteen young men gave their lives to Christ in a jail service. Of course, I don't know what effect this will have on my career as a chaplain, but then that's not my business. I praise God I have learned that it's all *His* business.

My Comments

Steps in praise lead to all kinds of fascinating experiences. We can never guess how God is going to work or what He is going to do. Many people step into the Baptism in the Holy Spirit when they start praising God for what is happening in their lives. I hope you are rejoicing in the knowledge that hundreds of military chaplains are now receiving the Baptism in the Holy Spirit. A four-star Army general is going back and forth across the country telling chaplains they need to be baptized in the Holy Spirit. Unbelieving senior chaplains are being forced to stand back and let God do "His thing." Times are changing!

But ye shall receive power, after that the Holy Ghost is come upon you: and ye shall be witnesses unto me. (Acts 1:8)

Brother Not a Christian

Dear Sir,

I know that you must be right about praising God for everything. However, there is one thing that I am not able to praise God for. My brother is not a Christian and does not want to be. How can I thank God for this?

My Comments

You have two choices: you can thank God that your brother is not a Christian and does not want to be, or you can thank God that he is going to be a Christian. If you have asked God to bring your brother to Christ, your opportunity now is to think of him as coming to Christ. Let your faith be free to picture him as already belonging to God. To me, this is a much better answer, and I believe it is the real truth about praising God. Those who keep their eyes on what is bad, and out of God's will, may continue to live in fear. Those who place their confidence and trust in the promises that Jesus gave have a right to believe that God is answering their prayers, and can then thank God that He is answering.

And this is the confidence that we have in him, that, if we ask any thing according to his will, he heareth us: And if we know that he hear us, whatsoever we ask, we know that we have the petitions that we desired of him. (I John 5:14-15)

I Have Demons

Dear Chaplain,

My sister and brother-in-law are wonderful Spirit-filled Christians. My brother-in-law had gone to a seminar where there were wonderful Christian speakers. He called one day and told us about one of the classes he had attended on demonology. The next day I prayed for deliverance. I had no idea what to expect or anything, but two demons left me. I asked my brother-in-law if he would pray for more demons to come out. We had listened to the tapes he had brought home, and I knew there were many demons in me. He held a regular deliverance service, and many demons fled, but I knew not all of them had gone, for they had talked to him and told him they were many.

I have the names of two more demons in me — numerology and mistakes. I know Satan is really at work, because how can one person make so many mistakes, especially when I have received so many answers from the Lord and then turned around and done the wrong thing? I have praised the Lord for my mistakes, but how long does He try to direct a person — until He loses patience? I just feel so drained. After the last mistake, I just don't know anymore. I'm not even sure I was baptized in the Holy Spirit, because I trembled the same way when the demons were working in me.

My Comments

When attention has been centered in demons, demons can be seen in everything. I have observed hundreds of cases where there was an initial joy when demons were thought to be cast out of Christians, but each new problem brought up the same thought: "I must have another demon in me. Where can I find someone to cast it out?" This eventually leads to loss of faith, discouragement, and defeat.

Demon activity is real — let there be no doubt of this. But we have received victory through Jesus. The disciples cast evil spirits out of people so they would be free to accept Jesus as their Savior. Then, with Christ within, they, too, had the authority to fight against Satan who was now on the outside. It is very important to recognize where Jesus is and where Satan is. Any misconception fills men with fear and eventually with doubt, even of their own salvation.

Rejoice not, that the spirits are subject unto you; but rather rejoice, because your names are written in heaven. (Luke 10:20)

A Doubting Thomas

Dear Reverend Carothers,

Praise the Lord for people like you! Several weeks ago I was stricken with a severe allergic reaction to a strep infection. I was hospitalized because my legs were so inflamed I couldn't walk. After nine days, there was no improvement — in fact, I was getting worse. Finally the doctor arrived early on Saturday afternoon and told me they could try one more type of medication, and if that didn't work, they didn't know what they were going to do. The new medication would be started at midnight. Needless to say, I was scared. But I had just finished reading *Prison to Praise,* so I laid back on my pillow and in my own simple way gave myself over to the Lord. I kept telling Him how much I trusted Him.

Within fifteen minutes, all the swelling and pain had left, and I started walking! I felt a peacefulness I have never known before in my life. This was before the new medicine was even started.

I have several friends, active in prayer groups, who tried to explain to me many times how easy it was to give one's life over to the Lord, but I was a doubting Thomas. I felt I had to know so much more and study so much more before I would be ready, and yet without my realizing what was happening, the Lord made it so easy for me.

I feel my stay in the hospital was the greatest gift our Lord could have given me. He certainly knows what He is doing. I am now reading your third book and can't put it down. Many of my friends are going to be recipients of your books for Christmas. God love you and take care of you every minute of your life.

My Comments

Many complicated, involved solutions to healing are being advocated by many well-meaning people (and some not so well-meaning). Healing comes by faith in God as revealed through Christ. If you are tempted to declare, "I have believed, but God has not done His part," please read this carefully. Having the faith in God that Jesus taught us to have is the most simple act in the world. But we have become very complicated by our very presence in the world! If you can admit that your own humanity is at fault, and never God, you open the door for the Holy Spirit to bring forth healing. If healing does not come instantly, do not immediately cry, "It doesn't work." Say, "God is healing me as He helps me to give up my doubting." If anyone asks you, "How are you?" declare to them, "Gloriously wonderful." Why say this? If you believe in your heart that God is healing you, then you have the right and the responsibility to rejoice in that healing.

If thou shalt confess with thy mouth . . . and . . . believe in thine heart . . . (Rom. 10:9)

Brain Surgery

Dear Chaplain Carothers,

Praise the Lord! I just thought I'd write and let you know what happened after I read *Prison to Praise* in April of this year. I was scheduled for brain surgery to relieve some of my involuntary movement in my left side.

I have had cerebral palsy ever since I had a whooping cough shot. I read your book the day before I went into surgery. I had such pain in my head after surgery, I really thought I was going to die! When my headache was so bad I couldn't stand it, I'd praise God for my pain. It would go away just like that. The minute I'd start feeling sorry for myself and say, "Oh God, why are you letting this happen to me?" the pain would come back even worse than it was before!

The Lord has been so good to me. As I write this, I am filled with peace and completely without pain.

My Comments

Sorry for myself — a common failure! This sorrow holds back deliverance. This beautiful example of how God works should stimulate every reader's faith. In this case, the pain was so intense that God brought instant deliverance when this young lady praised Him. In many cases, pain has to flee instantly when we praise God *for* the pain as it is. In other stituations, He brings peace that enables us to rejoice in His love, and the joy overcomes the pain.

A Blind Girl

On a Saturday evening about ten o'clock, I received a telephone call asking me if I could talk to a girl who was blind and needed encouragement desperately. The caller indicated that the girl would probably kill herself before morning unless someone helped her. I said that I would talk with her, although my natural inclination was to say that I couldn't at that late hour.

After the telephone conversation, I confess that a grumbling spirit tried to control my mind. I thought of the four services I would have the next day, how late it was, and about the prospect of receiving people that night at eleven o'clock. I also thought about the early hour I would be compelled to get up on Monday morning in order to fly from California to Florida.

"Oh, Lord, will I have the strength to do all of this?" I prayed. The Spirit said, "If you will praise Me and thank Me, you will experience something wonderful from this."

I couldn't think of anything wonderful that might happen, but determined to be truly and completely thankful for this late caller. I rejoiced and thanked the Lord for the coming opportunity to minister to someone in need. My spirit responded in thanksgiving and praise.

The people did not arrive until about 11:30 P.M. I held both hands of the blind girl and led her into our living room. After sharing my faith in God's power to heal her, I felt urged by the Spirit to place my hands on her head and pray a positive prayer for her healing. When I was through praying, I was directed to make a bold step of faith. I said, "Now open your eyes and tell me what you see."

"I see you right in front of me!"

I opened my Bible and held it in front of the girl. She read from a fine-print Bible, word for word, and I knew that God had performed a miracle.

If I had permitted a spirit of grumbling to overwhelm my

spirit of praise and thanksgiving, I would have prohibited God from doing what He wanted to do.

There have probably been many instances in your own life in which God could have powerfully changed many situations that surround you if you had known the secret of thanking Him for everything. Hindsight is often better than foresight, but you will never know what God will do until you follow His Word and thank Him for the slightest detail in your life.

What Should I Eat

Dear Reverend Carothers,

How can I praise the Lord when everything I eat causes me intense pain? The doctors cannot find anything wrong with me, but I keep on suffering. Should I stop eating? Should I lie and say I feel good when I don't?

My Comment

With infinite care, people observe their body, and react to its slightest symptom. When the body says, "I feel good," they react in joy. When the body says, "I feel bad," they react in sadness or fear. The body becomes the center of attention! It heaps demands upon demands. Anxious attention is placed on "What should I eat? What should I not eat?"

When we have given our body over to Him, it becomes His responsibility! Matthew 6:25 says, "Take no thought for your body." At one time I had at least 100 foods that made me ill. *Now, nothing does.* Satan learned that every time he used food to distress me, I praised the Lord for the distress! This cleared the way for God to heal me! You can find freedom through praise.

Seven Christian Friends

Dear Brother Carothers,

I do not know how to thank you enough for your prayers. I wrote and asked you to pray that God would help me to find some Christian fellowship here in prison. You wrote and told me that God would soon supply me with seven Christian friends. It was difficult for me to believe this, for there seemed to be no Christian men at all here. But you were right, and God has answered your prayers. I soon had six Christian friends, and then seven, and the number has grown. Now I can rejoice, and praise the Lord for the wonderful things He is doing. Could you send me an additional six copies of *Prison to Praise?* There are more men here who need to read it.

I was going to send this letter to you yesterday, but was delayed, and since then we have been able to lead two more men to Christ. It is nearly unbelievable to see what God is doing. Thank you for sending us the first copies of *Prison to Praise,* for they have indeed changed my life, and now the lives of many men.

My Comment

God is reaching into all levels of society and drawing members of His Body together. The mighty power of the Holy Spirit is revealing through prophecy and words of knowledge the needs of men in all places. Whatever your position in life, the Holy Spirit wants to use you to reach out and touch the needs of others. You may not even dream of the powerful way that God could use you if you would let the Holy Spirit lead you. He is only interested in using those who want to be led by His Spirit. As you read this, open your heart, and ask the Holy Spirit to lead you into whatever ministry God has designed for you. If the answer coming to you does not seem like something very glamorous or exciting, do not refuse to listen to the Spirit's leading. God has His plan, and even though your part may seem small and unimportant to you, in God's eyes the slightest obedience on your part will bring tremendous results.

From a Nun

Dear Mr. Carothers,

I can't thank you enough for the copies you sent to me of *Prison to Praise.* I shall pass them on to those in need. I am sure they will do good. Thanks to you, I am happy, happy, happy and at peace. You helped me find the real Christ.

My Comments

What kind of faith have you found? Your religion may have given you a sense of peace because it satisfies your own desire to "do something good," but has it made you "happy, happy, happy"? The very fruit of the Holy Spirit is joy. Rejoice that you have been born where you have heard the glorious Good News of what Jesus Christ came to the world to do for you. Rejoice in every thought. Rejoice that you do not know what to rejoice about! Rejoice that you are rejoicing without knowing what it is all about. Think no thought that is not a rejoicing thought, and the Holy Spirit will work His miracle in you!

God that made the world and all things therein . . . hath made of one blood all nations of men to dwell on all the face of the earth, and hath determined the times . . . and the bounds of their habitation; That they should seek the Lord, if haply they might feel after him, and find him. (Acts 17:24, 26-27)

Two Wayward Sons

Dear Reverend Carothers,

I have been reading your books and have been trying to believe that something good is going to happen to my two sons. I have raised them to believe in God and have taken them to church since they were babies. They have refused to accept Christ, and have now left home. I do not know where they are or what they are doing. How can I be thankful that they may be doing something wrong or may even be in jail, or a hospital? I would appreciate any help you can give me.

My Answer

Before your sons left, did you ask God to win them to Christ? Did you ever ask Him to do whatever is necessary to help them accept Christ? If you did, are you willing to let God win them His way, or will you insist that He do it your way? If you are willing to let God win your boys to Christ in His own way, He will surely answer your prayers. God is bound by His own promises to you, but He can do only what you trust Him to do.

I strongly recommend that you believe God is using the present position of your boys to lead them to Christ. This means that you must turn them over to Him and believe that He is carefully taking care of all that is necessary. They may need to go through difficult experiences, but surely this is better than never having any trouble and in the end dying without knowing the Lord Jesus.

My Comments

So many people are doing their best to find a reason why they should not praise God for this or that. People would be so much better off if they would follow Christ's admonition to believe and to trust in God. Your faith may be weak, but it will never grow as long as you persist in keeping your eyes on the problem rather than centering your attention on believing that God is working out the perfect solution to your need.

From a Jewish Girl

Dear Chaplain,

I am so glad God led me to purchase *Praise* (a combination book). What richness comes from a "positive praise life"!

My mother has never confessed Christ as Messiah and Savior. This bothered me constantly (Satan had a field day) until I praised God for her love for me that never ceased. I am at perfect peace concerning Mom (and all my family), knowing He does inhabit the praises of His people.

My Comments

Christians all too often live in torment over the spiritual condition of their loved ones. They are driven to feel that it would be wrong for them to carry anything less than a heavy burden for those they love. This is one of Satan's most clever tricks. He uses our "burden" to rob us of Christ's joy. If we were overflowing with joy, God would use this joy to increase our faith in Him. Our faith would release God's power to work in our loved ones.

Jesus did the weeping. He claimed the victory! We are to rejoice in what *He is doing* for those we love. If this lovely Jewish girl can believe for her family, you can!

P.S. Since receiving her first letter, I've learned that the girl's mother is going to church with her now!

I Refused

Dear Mr. Carothers,

The Lord called me to serve Him forty years ago. I refused. I can see now that many people could have been helped if I had not been so insistent that I do what I wanted to do. I cannot see any reason to thank God that I turned Him down. It bothers me every time I think about it. Can you help me?

My Answer

Your mistake will continue to hurt you, and the blessing you could have been to the world will never happen unless you thank God that He will take your mistakes, and use them to help others. Give thanks that He *is* doing it, and He *will.* He promised to! I knew a man in your situation who turned his problem over to God and was quickly filled with an amazing joy. When he spoke to young people about the mistake he had made in choosing his life's work, they wept openly. Many of these young people have now gone into full-time Christian work as a direct result of this man's realization that God would use him where he was.

In that man's case, it is easy to see the benefits of praising God for ourselves as we are, but in others it is not so evident. It is not our job to see the evidence! Our responsibility is to believe that God will take our life, as it is, and use everything we have done, or not done, to build His Kingdom. If you want to waste the rest of your life feeling sorry for your mistakes, that is your choice. I can tell you that it does not have to be that way! Praise Him for your mistakes, believe that He has been and will continue working them for your good, and you will experience a release of your spirit.

Praise and Thanks

Dear Reverend Carothers,

It may seem like an unimportant question, but I really would like to know the difference between praise and thanks. Or is there a difference?

My Answer

To many people, there definitely is a difference between praise and thanks. To some, praise means saying words of praise to God because they are afraid not to. To some, it means praising God because it is the thing we are supposed to do. They are being obedient to what they believe, but this is not thanks-giving. Giving thanks to God is not the traditional, "Thank you for passing the butter." It is any inward joy and gladness that God is doing what He is doing for His own perfect reasons. It is a heartfelt faith that He who loves us is putting His love into practice.

Many people have told me, "I can't be honestly thankful. What should I do?"

My reply is, "Go ahead and praise God as much as you are able. Be honest. Tell Him, 'Lord, You know I don't really thank You, but I'm willing to!' God will honor this, and His Spirit will help your thanksgiving to grow. Believe that Christ is being thankful within you. He was, and is, and always will be thankful to God. He will be the same within you. Satan may be right when he says, "You are not really thankful." Don't argue the point with him. Declare that Christ within you is thankful. You are in Him, and He is in you, and together you are one! Satan can not deny Christ's faithfulness! Your praise and thanksgiving will blend into one, and you will be praising and giving thanks.

At that day ye shall know that I am in my Father, and ye in me, and I in you. (John 14:20)

Be Thankful and Still Ask

Dear Chaplain Carothers,

I have read your books about being thankful and still praying for what we desire, but I still cannot understand it. How can we honestly be thankful for what we are, and have, and still ask God to change things? If you possibly have the time, please answer me.

My Answer

Your question is not unusual. I am asked this very frequently. Our prayers to God are usually governed by the depth of our spiritual relation with Him. We may begin by asking Him only for "things." This may not be the highest type of prayer, but He often honors it to help our faith. Later, the Holy Spirit urges us forward to ask for spiritual blessings and to trust God to supply whatever material things we really need. In my own life, I have discovered that when I seek for more of His love in my heart, He has given me material blessings that I would never have dreamed of asking for. This reveals to me that our prayers for "things" are not really necessary. He knows exactly what we want, and need, and will give them to us without our asking if we are so busy praising Him we don't get around to asking Him!

Physical needs of your own or of those you love may be so great that you feel compelled to plead with Him for deliverance. Often this deliverance does not come, because we are actually blaming God for not coming to our assistance. It would be against His own laws to reward such prayers. These resentments may be so deep sometimes that we don't know we have them. Praise and thanksgiving to God can and will uproot the resentments and open the doors for God to give us what He wants us to have.

You can pray like this: "Lord, I know You love me. Whatever You have permitted in my life must be somehow for my good. My sickness has been painful, but I know You are using it to help me. Thank you for helping me even when I haven't realized it. But you have also given me a desire to be well (or for my loved ones to be well), and so I ask You to give me health."

Now you have fitted your desires and His will into one. The resentments leave, and the Holy Spirit will help you to believe. You can never have healing faith unless the Holy Spirit helps you, and He will not help you if you are resentful over what God has permitted.

My Comments

Many people are bound by their resentments. God has constructed your body in such a way that resentments make you ill. Is it any mystery that He has constructed the power of faith so that resentments hold back faith? Find release from resentments, and faith will flow within you.

The children of Israel wanted desperately to get to the Promised Land. They probably prayed for forty years to enter in, but only two out of millions made it. Why? They kept grumbling because God wasn't doing things the way they thought He should.

God loved You too much to let His Own Chosen Race be a poor example to you. You can clearly see that they couldn't receive an answer to their prayers because they resented the way God was leading them. Can you think of prayers God hasn't answered for you? If so, look back from whence you have come, and begin to praise Him for all he has let you (and yours) go through.

God Blessed My Son

Dear Chaplain Carothers,

My son was a nearly perfect example of a good son. He was a fine Christian in every sense of the word. He was a loving husband and a real father to his children. In his church and community he was respected as an outstanding example.

Then his job began to fall apart. The business that employed him steadily declined, and he was able to work less and less. When he was down to working two days a week, he had to sell his beautiful home. He kept believing God would help him, and found a business he could get into with the equity he received from the sale of his house. We all prayed and believed that this was the reason his job had become so poor. We praised the Lord for giving him this new very prosperous-looking business opportunity.

But then the business venture fell through, and he was not able to even get started. Our faith was at a low ebb. Then we found *Prison to Praise* in our local bookstore. We joined in thanking God for the whole thing as it was. A completely unexpected thing happened, something we had never dreamed of. God spoke to my son and told him he was to enter full-time Christian work. The guidance came clear and positive. Our eyes were open. We saw clearly what it was God wanted to do. Now we are rejoicing that we learned to trust Him and make it possible for Him to do His will.

My Comments

Very often God's perfect plan for our lives, and the lives of those we love, is blocked by our lack of faith in His promise to work things for our good. True, He can later use even our failure, but why should you suffer and agonize when you never need to? He wants you to enjoy the benefits now!

I Resented My Weakness

Dear Colonel Carothers,

For more years than I can remember, I resented my physical weakness. I kept thinking of how many more things I could do for God if I didn't become exhausted so quickly. There was a very evident physical cause for my weakness, and I prayed daily to be healed. I steadily tried to believe that God completely healed me through Christ, but the physical weakness continued, and grew worse with age.

Then I read *Prison to Praise.* It seemed ridiculous to be thankful for my weakness, but I tried. I could think of several benefits it had brought throughout my life, but this never overbalanced the anxiety of wanting to do more for God. Then my praise started taking effect. I was soon believing that God had me the way He could use me best. A new joy over "me as I was" grew inside. I learned to like the "me" that I was. With this came a gradual yet quickening change in my body. I noticed that I was feeling less and less tired. Praise the Lord for what has happened to me.

My Comments

This person's physical body might not have received this new strength through thanksgiving, but it did. In her case, God wanted her to praise Him so He could manifest His strength in her weakness. If you have a physical, emotional, or mental weakness, praise God for "you" as you are. He will take your praise and lift you to new heights in whatever way He desires for you. If you expect what has happened to others, you may be disappointed. Expect what He wants for you, and I promise you, you will always be thoroughly and completely satisfied!

I Didn't Mean It

Dear Sir,

I prayed, "God I believe You and will trust You to work this thing out for good."

But I knew I didn't mean it at all. I didn't believe God would work it out. The situation has grown increasingly worse for many years, and regardless of how I pray, it gets more painful all the time. If I tell God I believe He will work this thing out for good, it is just plain lying. What do I do?

My Answer

Be completely honest with God. Plainly say, "I want to trust You, but I cannot believe You are going to help change this terrible situation. I ask You to help me believe! I ask for Christ to believe in me what I cannot believe myself. I believe He is able to believe You for anything."

If you are able to believe that Christ will believe within you, then you can honestly say, "In Christ I am believing." Then you can believe that since He is trusting for you, God is now able to work the whole thing out for good.

Your admission that you cannot believe yourself is actually a greater blessing to you than if you were immediately able to believe yourself! As you see Christ believing in you, you will give Him credit rather than your own faith.

His Reply

Dear Sir,

Your advice kind of floored me at first. It sounded good, but I didn't think I could do it. Ministers had given me all kinds of advice before, but I had never heard of letting Christ believe for me. As soon as I believed that He would believe for me, I immediately felt as if a burden had left me. I wasn't guilty anymore because I couldn't believe God.

I started to laugh inside as if I was free. This was great, but what happened next was even greater. The problem I had showed immediate signs of improving. I was still afraid to believe that God was doing anything, but I kept believing Christ would believe for me. The problem kept getting better. At times, I have held my breath in amazement. Now I myself believe! I know God has worked a miracle in my life. I'm still amazed that God has done this for me.

My Comment

I rejoice that this child of God is now able to believe Him. His faith has grown. He knows that Christ is to receive the credit! He will tell others, and they will be encouraged to believe. Their faith will reach others. Every time we take a step of faith, others will be helped by our faith just as our faith is helped by Christ! But He will receive all the credit, for we will say in unison, "To Him be the glory."

I can do all things through Christ which strengtheneth me. (Phil. 4:13)

Epilepsy

Dear Brother Carothers,

I was having epileptic seizures every week of my life. Only those who have lived with this disease know the horror it brings. After I knew Jesus as my Savior, I was less unhappy, but the seizures continued. When I heard about praising the Lord *for* my sickness, it sure didn't make any sense to me. How could I, a young person, be thankful for this horrible thing?

But I started praising the Lord, and faith grew in me that He was healing me. The seizures decreased in frequency and intensity. Jesus *was* healing me. I stopped taking my medicine and still felt well. When my parents found out about the medicine, they were very upset and tried to get me to go back on it. I begged them to let me continue as I was. They then insisted that I had to go to the doctor to see what he said.

I was given a brain-wave test and fully expected the results to be negative. I was surprised when the doctor said there was still very positive evidence that my brain was suffering from epilepsy and that I had to go back on my medication right away. I said, "But why haven't I had any seizures for several months if I am still so ill?" He had no explanation for this, but said I was sure to have continued attacks.

I was really confused. What should I do? My parents were now even more insistent that I go back to my medicine. In prayer, I felt a returning peace, and a certainty that God was healing me. I again begged my parents to let me stay off the medicine until they saw the first positive evidence that I had to have it. To this, they finally agreed.

This was over a year ago! I have taken no medicine and have enjoyed perfect health. Thank the Lord for teaching me to praise Him, and trust Him. Your books on praise have greatly fortified my faith, and I thank you for helping me to enjoy the great blessing of health.

My Comment

Very often I am asked, "Should I stop taking my medicine if I am believing God to heal me?" I always say, "Let the Holy Spirit guide you. Only He knows how God wants to heal you." Those who make rash statements, such as, "You should never take medicine for any reason," are completely wrong. This advice, to those who do not have the faith for healing, can bring unnecessary pain and suffering to God's people. When the Holy Spirit gives us the faith to believe that we are well, *that* is the time to stop taking medicine. When *that* time comes, you will not need to ask any human being what you should do. He will make it clear to you, and your health will be perfect.

A Catholic Sister Writes to Other Catholic Sisters

Dear Sisters,

I have some good news I want to share with you. For thirty years my full-time work has been teaching people how to get to heaven, but it was not until a few weeks ago that I found out how easy it is.

One evening I was talking to Sister Rose, and she showed me a book called *Prison to Praise.* She gave me all kinds of reasons why I should read it. All the time she was trying to convince me, I was thinking about all the work I had to do in my bookkeeping office; the things I had to prepare for my first communion class; and besides that, I was supposed to help with the spring housecleaning here at the convent. However, I took the book — just to be polite. The next day I decided I better read a few pages, just so I could tell Sister Rose I had started it. I found it so exciting I could not put it down.

The author, Mr. Merlin Carothers, was in the Army, and he was also in prison a few times. I won't take time to tell you about all the crimes he committed. He was a very intelligent man and the FBI had a hard time catching him. When he got out of prison, he was almost a millionaire, and still a very young man. He had made his money in a dishonest way, but the FBI had not found out about that.

Mr. Carothers made the mistake of going to visit his grandmother on a Sunday afternoon. She wanted him to go to church with her that evening. He said he couldn't go because one of his friends was coming to pick him up. This was a big lie. He got on the phone and tried to call all of his friends to ask someone to pick him up, but nobody happened to be home, so he had to go to church with his grandmother. He thought, "What a foolish way to spend a Sunday evening when there are so many exciting things to do." Soon after he got in church, he could not help but notice how happy these people were — much happier than he was, in spite of his money. That night God changed his life, and God filled this criminal with his grace and love. Soon after, he became an Army chaplain, and he went back to the very same place he had been a handcuffed prisoner.

Chaplain Carothers found out that the most powerful prayers are prayers of praise and thanksgiving. (Most of us are always saying prayers of "Give me this" and "Give me that.") He also studied the Bible and began to realize that God, the most loving of Fathers, has planned every detail of our lives with the most loving care. The chaplain tells about many people who came to him for advice about their problems. He told these people that God had permitted their problems to happen and would bring good out of them if they would praise and thank God for them. Naturally, he had great difficulty convincing most people that this was true, but once they praised and thanked God for their problems, great things did happen!

All types of people came to the chaplain: some were very sick, others were in deep depression, some on the verge of committing suicide. He told them God loves them, and God would bring good out of these things if they would praise and thank Him for them. Many of these people said, "But I have never done very much for God. I really don't deserve to have God do anything for me. He told them that was very true. None of us deserve to receive God's gifts, but God does not give us His gifts because we deserve them. He gives us His gifts because He loves us. All we have to do is to believe that He loves us and trust Him. It is easy to trust God when everything is going fine, but it is very hard to trust Him when we have serious illness, are in a car accident, out of work, etc. God, our loving Father, tells us in the Bible that these things, too, have been permitted by Him, and if we trust Him, He will bring good out of them.

It makes me very sad when I meet so many people who think it is hard to get to heaven. These people are traveling the road of fear when they should be traveling the road of love. The road of love is so easy, for when we realize that God, our loving Father, loves each one of us with a personal infinite love, we can't help but love Him. God's love for you is a million times greater than the love of any mother for her child.

These books filled me with such joy and peace, I just had to tell you about them. There is only one difficulty about reading these books: most people who read them want to buy one for each of their friends, and this could be rather expensive.

I hope I have convinced you that you should read these books, but just in case I haven't, I dare you to read them. I guarantee you that you will be amazed at the happy results.

My Comments

With publicity like this, the *Praise* books will reach into the farthest corners of the world! Thank you, Sister, for believing enough to do something to share your belief with others. There is no greater stimulus to your own enthusiasm than sharing with others whatever God has shared with you. Jesus made it clear that God will not continue to give you His blessings if you hide them within yourself.

Neither do men light a candle, and put it under a bushel, but on a candlestick; and it giveth light unto all that are in the house. (Matt. 5:15)

Try Harder — More Trouble

Dear Reverend Carothers,

We desperately need your prayers. We have so many problems, I don't even know where to begin to tell you about them. If you ask the Lord, I know He will tell you what they are.

My husband drinks all of the time. For fifteen years he drank a lot, but now it is all the time he is off work. He loves his friends, but has no time for his family. He thinks his friends are perfect, and there is nothing good about us. His hatred caused our very young daughter to get pregnant by a boy of another color. The boy wants to marry her, but my husband will not permit it.

You wouldn't believe how many times my husband has beaten me. This only happens when he is drunk, but since he is drunk all the time, I live in fear. I have tried with all my heart to be a good wife, but nothing I do is right. I want us to go to church and have a Christian family, but he won't go.

When he beats me, he is usually sorry the next day and tells me he will never do it again. Then he acts as if he loves me, and I know I do love him. Regardless of what he does, I can't help but love him. It breaks my heart to see our lives and family being thrown away. I've asked God to take him out of my heart, but he is still there.

I got away from the God I knew when I was a young girl, but I know He is still there. The harder I try to get close to Him, the more troubles we have. Please tell me what to do.

My Answer

Your problem is different from the ones many people have, but the cause is the same. In some cases it is difficult to see why people have to go through such frustration, but in a situation like yours, it is easier to see what is happening. You write, "The harder I try to get closer to Him, the more

58

troubles we have." Any time anyone tries to get closer to God, the devil will rear his ugly head. His *business* is to fight against people who want to get close to God. The weapons he uses are many, but the plan is the same. If he can keep our eyes on our problem, he can keep our eyes off God! You can turn the tables on him by thanking God for whatever is happening.

Believe that you are getting close enough to God to give Satan cause to worry. It may hurt to think of Satan using your own husband to fight against you, but remember that Satan can use anyone who will let him. You can break free and trust God to use your husband to *help* you. This will also help your husband! Your faith in God will release God's power to help your entire family.

Thou hast caused men to ride over our heads; we went through fire and through water, but thou broughtest us out into a wealthy place. (Ps. 66:12)

My Comments

Many people find it difficult to believe in a being called the devil. I thank the Lord for having let me go far enough away from Him that I came to know the devil for the very personal being he is. His presence and activity in this world is as real as that of any person you will ever know. If you disbelieve in him, you will be unaware of what he is doing.

But we do not have to live in fear of the devil. Far too many people are now spending most of their time casting out evil spirits. We are victorious only in Christ. We are completely victorious in Him. If you believe you have an evil spirit in you, your faith will be so weakened, you will live in fear. If you believe Jesus lives within you, and Satan is fighting on the outside, you will grow in faith and confidence. The man known as "Mr. Pentecost" throughout the charismatic movement, David du Plessis, declares that it is impossible for an evil spirit to live inside a body that Jesus lives in. He says, "We are the temple of God and not the home for Satan." I agree with him.

59

For Others

Dear Sir,

I have heard several authors speak, and as far as I am concerned, they were just plain blah. From beginning to end, I didn't know what they were talking about.

When I went with my parents to hear you, I wasn't looking forward to it. "Another writer?" I wailed.

I tried to get set as comfortably as possible to endure whatever of your ideas you might be expounding upon. But when you opened your mouth, you immediately got my attention. I could see you really believed in what you were talking about. I relaxed and decided to listen for at least a little while.

The longer you talked, the more interested I got. You seemed so happy, I started feeling happy myself. I realized I was sitting on the edge of the pew trying not to miss a word. Your ideas on praising God were certainly unique, but you sort of pulled mc in. As you poured out one illustration after another about the power of praise, I became more and more interested. Your enthusiasm and excitement were really catching!

I didn't have any real big problems in my own life, but I started thinking what your ideas could do to help the people who are really busted on life. I've always wanted to do something to help other people, but I had never thought of anything that *I* could actually do.

By the end of your message, I was really high. I could see that most of the people were excited, too. Even then I was amazed at the number of people who went forward when you gave an invitation. Most of them were weeping, and I've never seen anything like that in my church.

But what happened that night isn't the reason I'm writing. When I went to college the next day, I decided I was going to put your ideas into practice. When anything happened that seemed a little unpleasant, I said out loud, "Praise the Lord" (but usually not very loud). It worked! I kept feeling better all day. I was excited over my discovery.

The next day I started saying, "Praise the Lord," loud enough for other people to hear it. They usually laughed at me, but I noticed that when they mimicked me, they had smiles on their faces. Several of them said, "Praise the Lord" to me when we passed in the halls. I knew they were sort of making fun of me, but I also saw we were becoming better friends. Then some of these same kids wanted to talk with me about "this new kick I was on." When I explained it, they were not convinced, but I asked them to really give it a try. Several have already told me they are being changed into happier people. Some of them haven't accepted Christ yet, but the door is opening, and I'm at last getting the chance to do something for others.

My Comments

To do something for others — this is a powerful need in every Christian's heart. He feels the desire but doesn't know what to do. Here is something you can get your teeth into. Every time something unpleasant happens to you, say, "Praise the Lord." Do it at home first. Instead of your usual grumble when you have to do something you prefer to not do, give a hearty "Praise the Lord."

You may not feel like praising the Lord, but do it anyhow. (God won't hold back the blessing because you don't feel like it.) When others see and hear your happy responses, they will be drawn to respond as you do. God will bless them and you!

Disc Jockey

Dear Chaplain Carothers,

We were introduced to the concept of praising God for all things over a year ago when we read *Prison to Praise*. My husband and I already believed that "all things work together for good" and that Christians must continue to praise God *in* all circumstances, but praising God *for* all circumstances was an entirely new idea to us. At the time we were having difficulties with our rebellious fifteen-year-old son, and we began to praise the Lord for each manifestation of his rebellion.

To make a long and very painful story short, as things seemed to get progressively worse, with each day bringing a major crisis, we gave up in despair and placed our son in a residential treatment center. At this point we re-read *Prison to Praise* and *Power in Praise*. Convinced that this was the only pathway to victorious living, we began again to thank God for our son exactly as he is. Again the crises came thick and fast.

On a Friday night, we faced a particularly hard praise challenge and called my sister to join us in a little prayer chapel to praise and pray. We left there with some measure of peace and a determination to continue to praise, but still no real joy.

The next morning, I was home alone when the phone rang. It turned out to be a disc jockey on the local "rock" radio station, offering me the money in their cash jackpot if I could tell him the exact amount of money in it. I told him my two teenagers were gone, that by choice I never listened to his station and had no idea how much money was in his pot. He told me I had just lost $1,057.55.

Well, I hung up and began to praise the Lord for the loss of $1,057.55. The more I praised the Lord, the more genuine my praise became; and the more I thought about what would have happened had the kids been home to answer the phone

62

(they probably would have known the amount), the more jubilant I became.

By the time my husband came home, an hour and a half later, I was skipping through the house. I told him what had happened. It took a minute for him to get on my wave length, as our year's expenses with psychiatrists, psychologists, etc., for our son have been astronomical, and $1,057.55 did sound pretty good, but soon he began to praise, too. It was the first time we had ever been called by a radio station and the first time we had ever had an opportunity to win money. Just as he said, "Well, if the Lord had wanted you to have it, you would have known the amount," the phone rang. When my husband answered, he turned to me and asked, "How much was that we didn't win?" I said, "$1,057.55," and he repeated it into the phone. Then he came back and sat down.

"We just won $1,057.55," he said.

"We what?"

"Yes. It was the same radio station with another disc jockey calling."

Two calls in one day when we had never had one such call before in our entire lives. It was His sweet assurance that He was pleased by our praise for adversity, and it bolstered our faith so that we could continue, if necessary, without immediate evidence of changes in the important situation.

I would like to report that we have not wavered since then, but the going is still rough. We know He is working things out perfectly, but we know it only by faith, and our praise is still sometimes tearful.

My Comments

One day we as Christians will realize that God has His own will and does His work in the way He wants to do it. Please do not read the above letter and think, "I wish God would give me $1,000 to meet my needs." Thank Him that He is meeting your needs in exactly the right way. He knows exactly what is best for the eternal spirit that lives within you. Jesus said that getting to heaven would be nearly

63

impossible for a rich man. The God who created you knows exactly the kind of spirit you have. If poverty is necessary to spare you from losing eternal life, God will see to it.

Do not misunderstand. I'm not saying that God wants everyone to be poor. Many people are poor only because of their own mistakes. I am saying that if you have done your very best to claim God's promises of prosperity and are still poor, God is providing what *you need.* Rejoice and be glad in it. Your praise may release your need, and God will then prosper you!

Praise Power

Dear Brother Carothers,

It was a real blessing to read *Answers to Praise,* apparently hot off the press. I was thinking how it must thrill you from the tip of your toes to the top of your head the way God is using you in this praise ministry.

It would take about 100 typewritten pages to cover the past year, but I'm condensing this testimony into a few basics. It is very exciting to me every time I see the miracle God performed in my life, and how it has affected lives around me.

For many years, I attended church, but there was always a wall between God and me — a wall I was afraid to break. Then, our Methodist church planned a lay-witness mission 3½ years ago. I managed to get involved in the planning, much to my dismay. What frightened me was that somehow I knew that during the mission I would make a commitment to God of some sort.

During the meetings, all the outsiders kept saying, "God loves you, and I love you." I felt terribly uncomfortable. During the final Sunday's message, I felt like the coordinator was looking straight through me. He had an altar call for those who wanted more of God in their lives — or something of that order. I found myself going forward, as if a magnet was drawing me. I didn't understand then that, according to Scripture, the Holy Spirit draws men to Christ. In fact, I'd never read the Bible at all. But the shell was broken, and I was open to learn.

About this time, our son became desperately ill with a paralytic disease. I spent hours weeping and sobbing, feeling that my world had caved in. Oh, that someone had told me about Christ and the victorious life through Him!

My mom arranged for us to visit a faith healer, a spiritualist. I didn't realize the dangers involved. After working with our son for a time, the healer had him walking across a room, the first steps in many months. She saw him a second time, and this time he felt electricity going through his body. But when we got back home, our son could not even crawl on his belly. He kept regressing until the paralysis affected his hands and even his optical nerves. I was desperate for help and thoroughly confused, as I had thought God healed him.

Next, I visited the Science of Mind church, knowing that several friends were quite happy there. I returned home with a book on "ultimate reality" — and all sorts of inner confusion and turmoil. I began to wonder who Jesus was, whether he was just a man, our example. I even began to wonder if God was real. Finally, I literally sobbed out, "God — if You are — I'm all confused and mixed up, and I don't know where to go or what to believe. Help me. Who is Jesus? Is He really God? I've got to know. Oh, help me." Boy! I didn't realize what I was asking for. Things began to happen. Fast.

At a luncheon, I heard about Jesus in a new way. A young couple giving their testimony really touched my heart, and I noticed the next day in church that I felt strangely exuberant.

After church I was at home in the bathroom just singing away, and I found myself singing out in funny sounds; almost like an opera. I was dumbfounded. Later, I was engrossed in a book on spiritual healing. As I read accounts of various healings, I had a funny sensation all over, and a torrent of words in a funny language kept pouring out of my mouth! I wondered what on earth was happening to me. Fortunately (God always arranges things so nicely!), I had the phone number of the luncheon leader. I contacted her and found out I most likely had received the Baptism in the Holy Spirit. She thought I must be speaking in tongues, but I had never heard of such a thing. I didn't realize, of course, that speaking in tongues brings edification and power.

Two weeks after this experience, my son was re-hospitalized 150 miles away from home. I tried to keep my chin up, but found myself dreadfully depressed and downtrodden. With three other handicapped children at home to care for, I became so exhausted, I could barely function. I thought of running away and never coming back. But I continued to attend the luncheons, which uplifted me a bit. Then it happened.

My friend invited me to a watch night New Year's Eve service at the Assembly. This was a foreign concept to me, attending church on New Year's Eve. But, no one had invited us to a party (Praise the Lord!) and I was in no shape to give one myself. So I dragged my husband along, and there we were, watching those funny people raise their hands in prayer. I thought, "Ye gads, what will my husband think of all this?" Then, I noticed he was playing follow the leader. I thought, "What the heck," lifted my own arms in praise, and the depression left like magic, never to return. I have been on cloud nine ever since, except for very short, intermittent periods, and they were my fault.

I learned that spiritism is of the devil and renounced all association with it. I began to realize that our son's false healing was Satanic. I praise God for opening my eyes to so much. I'd been taught that hell and Satan are not real – this is just self. I learned the truth in those areas, too. The hospital allowed our son to come home on a visit, and I felt impressed to arrange a genuine healing service at our church for him and others in need. I honestly believed that our son would hop right out of his wheelchair and run down the aisles, but he didn't move a muscle. God had much more for us to learn.

The next evening, the evangelist asked if any who fasted

and prayed for healings felt their prayers were not answered. Guess who jumped up. He had me place my hand on the Bible and claim God's healing promises. I fell prostrate for over an hour, and God spoke to me, saying, "He is healed; He is healed." Praise God for the gift of faith, as I never again doubted the healing, even though there was no visible evidence of it.

The hospital called me a few days later and chewed me out royally for taking my son out in public. Our paralyzed son, with little respiratory system left, was sick as a dog, running a high fever. I *knew* this was Satanic and rebuked Satan in the name of Jesus Christ and told him to get lost. "God tells me my son is healed, and I believe Him!" I said.

The next morning, our son could lift his legs, roll over in bed, and crawl on his hands and knees. He astounded everyone, and many of the staff looked frantically for logical reasons for the overnight recovery. After three weeks, he experienced another setback and the hospital sent him home. For three weeks, I cared for a paralyzed boy whose wheelchair weighs sixty-five pounds. It was rough to keep praising God, but because I *knew* my son was healed, I could ignore much of the problem. I never did feel burdened down, really.

Then sickness descended again. He caught the flu, but as we praised God for this, he began to improve by leaps and bounds. One day, he could partially dress himself; the next day he could climb into a tub, etc. This summer, he began walking a few steps. By August, he was riding a bike and climbing trees. He has everyone astounded! His wheelchair and all the trimmings have been donated to the school for handicapped children, as he can now climb right up the school bus steps without assistance. Praise God!

This is just one tiny portion of what God has done in my life the past few months. It is truly fantastic. I know no other word to describe all the emotional and physical healings we've experienced, the knowledge He's given to us of His Son, His Holy Word, and His personal love for each of us. I had asked God to reveal Himself to me. He continues to answer my prayer in mighty ways.

My Comments

Reading and answering piles of letters often exhausts me. I finished this letter with a song of joy and experienced new health in my own body. Has reading the letter done anything for you? If you have been wrestling with the problem of physical healing, I suggest you read the letter again and ask the Holy Spirit to give you special insight as to just how God worked in this case.

Guilty for Becoming Sick

Dear Pastor Carothers,

Since Jesus became a living reality in my life, and I have been filled with His Holy Spirit, I accepted Him as my Healer. Whereas I had previously had the normal colds, headaches, and physical aches that most elderly people have, I found a perfect health that gave life a new kind of joy. I shared this experience with many of my Christian friends and helped them to enter into health. Others didn't understand, but were thankful for what I had.

One morning I became violently ill, and was taken to the doctor by my husband. The doctor rushed me to the hospital. Several doctors there dropped what they were doing and prepared to operate on me. Everything happened so quickly, I could hardly believe it was me. My husband agreed with the doctors that I should have surgery.

I was shocked. How could I be physically ill when Jesus had so clearly made me well? I had lived in perfect peace that He would always supply all I needed, and yet I couldn't deny that I was violently ill, and had signs of approaching death. I agreed to the operation. They found a malignant cancer that they believed would have killed me that very day.

68

When I was recovered, and on the way back to complete health, my faith was in deep turmoil. Had I failed God? Would my friends' faith in God be shattered by my own failure? What should I tell them about an experience I didn't understand myself? I could find no rest, and in fact have still found no peace. I know I am God's child, but carry great guilt that I have failed Him so miserably.

My Comments

This kind of guilt and fear is growing in our Christian community. As God is bringing health and healing to many, others are falling into fear and condemnation. This fear is fed by those who boldly declare it is wrong to accept illness. Those who wisely and rightly share God's healing power are often unwise in not completing their ministry by sharing God's will for us to praise and thank Him. It is true that He does want us to be well, but it is also true that our spiritual weakness often keeps Him from healing us. Should we then lament our weakness and groan because of our failure? I do not believe so. Every time we fail, we are a testimony to one all-important fact. We are imperfect, but Christ is perfect. We need Christ to supply what we are not. Our very imperfection is a powerful reminder to us that we need Christ to supply what we can not do or be. This in itself is God's will. He wants to remind us in some way of our own weakness. Paul received so many powerful answers to prayer, yet he had to endure one thing that he had asked God to remove. This reminded him of his weakness, and kept him dependent upon Christ.

Of course, others may be wounded by our lack of perfect faith, but that is not our problem, it is His. He has accepted us as His and has admonished us, "Let not your heart be troubled: . . . believe" (John 14:1).

We should not now say, "I'll just accept all sickness that comes along," and not exert our faith to be well in Christ. We should reach out as far as we can, believe Him, and trust Him to take care of whatever problems develop. Most people are ill far more than their spiritual growth warrants, but many

69

people are also needlessly suffering from guilt. Guilt and condemnation never help faith to grow, but praise and thanksgiving will multiply our faith to receive whatever God knows we are ready to receive.

In Russia

Dear Brother Carothers,

In 1968 I had the opportunity to go to Moscow, Russia, as a tourist. On the second day there, during a guided tour, I fell and badly sprained my ankle. The pain was so terrific that I nearly passed out. The guide called for medical assistance, and an ambulance arrived with men in white coats. Through the translator, they told me I had an exceptionally bad sprain, and shouldn't put any weight on my leg. They bandaged it, which seemed to make it hurt worse.

When the men finished, I asked them where I could get crutches. They didn't know. They didn't even know where a cane could be purchased or borrowed. A friend with me asked if an ice pack would help my ankle. They said it might. No one offered to help me, so I hobbled over to our car and returned to the hotel. With agonizing pain I managed to get to our room.

My friend went downstairs to try to locate some ice, and aspirin, or any kind of pain killer. By this time, my leg was badly swollen, and when I took the bandage off, I could see the entire ankle was black and blue. The pain was so bad, I had to do something to get my mind off it. I thought of singing. The only song that came to my mind was "Praise God from Whom All Blessings Flow." Gritting my teeth, and singing at the same time, I did my best. By the end of the chorus, something very strange had happened to the ankle. The pain was gone! I stood up and walked around and laughed and laughed. The ankle was still swollen and black, but there was absolutely no pain.

70

When my friend came back, she couldn't believe me when I told her the pain was gone. The next morning, the ankle was still black, but the swelling had started to go down. Still no pain! No trace of pain ever came back to the ankle. I hadn't read *Prison to Praise* then and didn't know about the powerful force of praise, but now I understand why God touched me.

My Comment

What a powerful commentary on the power of praise! In this case, God used praise even though this woman intended it only to get her mind off her pain. What unlimited healing could be released in this world if we, God's children, would heed His recommendation to praise Him continually. Our praise is now being used by God to release a healing flow of His Love, and it is reaching round the world. The reservoir of power within you may lie dormant, but your praise and trust in God could release healing and life to many, many people. Grumbling, complaining, faultfinding is being released by Satan. This force pulls suffering and pain over the world like the moon pulls the ocean over the land. God will use your praise to set many captives free!

Ask God for Mercy

Only God knows what I have suffered — lung trouble, stomach trouble, heart trouble, severe dizziness, depression, weakness, and fear. Would you ask God to have mercy on me and heal me and take away this terrible fear? I was very sick all summer also with high blood pressure. My husband doesn't seem to want to help me.

I think all this trouble is the result of almost a lifetime of brooding over my husband's interest in other women. I also have a low blood sugar condition. I am forty-eight years old, and with all my sickness I don't know if I can carry on.

Ask God for His mercy? Never! He hasn't had any part in all this suffering! The devil is the one who causes sickness, fear, and depression. God gave His only Son to die for this woman, and she is killing herself. She is right! Like many people, she is brooding over some problem or other, and at the same time asking God to do something about her problem. God has already done His part. Jesus accepted our sicknesses and problems on the Cross. His part is complete! Oh, if people could only see this. God wants us to believe that through Jesus everything is already solved.

When this dear wife gives her husband and herself over to Jesus, she will be completely, and perfectly well. How should she do it? By beginning to thank God for her husband as he is and for herself as she is. When she rejoices that God is working out His perfect plan, she will at that moment be in perfect peace. Her physical problems will be as nothing compared to the peace she experiences within. This will automatically usher her into the health that Jesus has bought for her. It probably will not be instantaneous, but it will make a powerful thrust into the self-pity and anxiety she has labored under for so long.

One of the greatest needs of people is to realize that God has already answered our prayers through His Son. Our part is to now accept His gift. Of course, it isn't an easy thing for us to do, but we can start by accepting our life exactly as it is and believe that God is working out His perfect plan for us. He is!

I Feel Like Walking Pain

Dear Pastor Carothers,
I have received the Baptism in the Holy Spirit, but my life is still not victorious. Writing this is so painful. Not quite two

weeks ago, my beautiful seventeen-year-old son ran wildly out the door in below-zero weather, wearing only his undershorts and socks — hallucinating from a huge amount of LSD. When he was found, he had frozen to death. I am trying to praise God. I praised Him while the whole town was searching for our son and while he was actually dying. Now I don't know. Please tell me specifically how to praise God.

I feel so guilty. We failed our son in a million ways — when he needed us most. I know God forgives me, but I am having so much trouble forgiving myself. I feel like walking pain.

My Answer

Greetings in Jesus name.

The boy who ran out of the house was not guided by his own mind. His mind had been taken over by a drug. He was not even aware of what was going on.

The results of your son's death now depend on you. Of course, Satan meant it to destroy you, your faith, and your family. You can now defeat him and make his entire plan work for your son's good, your good, and the world's good. Believe that God is using the entire incident to work out good! Just as He used the senseless death of Jesus on the Cross, He can use your son's death to bring light and hope to thousands of young people and parents. How? By your faith. This is His promise. He will use everything for good *if* you trust Him. Remember, only *if* you will trust and praise Him.

Your son's death could profit nothing if nothing is done about it. Fear, anguish, self-pity, regrets, guilt, doubts — all fall right into Satan's plan. If you succumb to these things, you are being used just as your son was used. His temptation was LSD. Yours is guilt and fear and pain. They kill and destroy just as LSD does. You have been helpless to gain victory, just as your son was. God understands this, but He will use your faith to bring something glorious out of the whole thing! *He* will — not you! I will believe with you!

73

My Comment

"If God is for real, why didn't He answer my prayer? I asked Him to help someone, but He didn't do it. If I were God, I would have helped them." Have you ever felt like this? If so, your question is your answer. Man as an egotistical being wants God to be like He thinks God should be. Some men want God to destroy all other men who are different than they are. They honestly believe the world would be better off if only their kind were in existence. Many are positive that their own plan of creation and operating the world would be far superior to God's. If this attitude has crept into your thinking, do not be surprised if the God who loves you lets you go through all kinds of calamities until you realize how unwise you really are. A maximum score on an intelligence test would not put you one step closer to knowing and understanding a God who wants you to trust Him.

Your own idea of how God should be, may be very good and acceptable to you and to others. There may be nothing wrong with your conception, but the very best you can put together is a reflection of your humanity. God knows enough about humans to know that at their very best they have destroyed many perfect things that He created. He wants us not to trust in our human judgment, but to rely completely upon faith in His Son. Peter sank into the water when he formed his own conclusions about what should be happening. When he placed his hand in Christ's, he came back to the top. I have reached the place where I now prefer to trust in Christ rather than in my own idea of how things should be done. I am therefore free to praise Him for everything that happens to me. I may not see how it could possibly be for good, but I know I can trust His knowledge above my own.

I Was Shot

A young woman said to me at the close of a meeting, "A girl friend of mine received a copy of *Prison to Praise* from a friend who had received it from another friend. Your book changed my life. I tried to get my husband to read it, but he repeatedly refused. He was then involved in an accident in which he was shot with a gun four times."

She introduced me to her husband. He said, "I don't know why I wasn't interested in reading the book, but I just wasn't. After I was shot and was in the hospital, I had a little time to think. One bullet had gone through a lung. Another had torn away parts of six ribs. One went through my neck. I was really messed up. When my wife brought the book to me then, I agreed to read it. I was still very weak, for it had been only two days since the accident.

"As I read your book, I was absolutely amazed at the things God did in your life. By the end of it, I had started thanking Him that I had been shot. A voice inside me said, 'Okay you can stand up and walk now. You have learned what you needed to know.'

"I pulled the tubes and wires out of me and got up. When the nurses saw me, they started hollering, 'Get back in bed!'

'No, I can't,' I told them. 'God has made me well.'

"The doctors came and were so astonished they didn't know what to do. I was still very weak, but I got my clothes and went home. I had no pain and no problems from then on. Thank you for writing that book."

Four couples who knew this man and his wife stood around them saying, "Isn't it wonderful! God did this for him," and "I saw him in the hospital before he read your book." Their beaming faces told me more than their words did.

My Comments

Wonderful! Yes it is, and it is exactly what God wants to do for many people who have become bogged down in their problems. Problems are needed only until we learn what we needed to know. We are then free to go on to more important things.

We Were Happy

My life and the lives of my little girls were shattered six weeks ago when my husband walked out on us for another woman. He has always lived an extremely moral and high-principled life, but has no religious beliefs at all. When anyone tries to witness to him, he strongly resents it. We've had a happy marriage, or at least I thought it was happy until this happened. The woman says she loves him and he loves her. He is going to file for divorce. We've had little things in our marriage that have always made it seem extra-special. We were both virgins when we became as one, and we've never even left one another for a brief errand without kissing each other good-bye.

The one major thing missing from our marriage has been God. I was reared very religiously, but drifted away from God in my college years, and I could feel a void in my life, but didn't know exactly what it was. Since my husband has been gone, I have re-dedicated my life to God, and feel closer to Him than I have in a long time. Even with the closeness to God, though, I get so despondent and depressed that I've even thought of taking my life.

A friend of mine loaned me your book *Prison to Praise* and I received a great inspiration from it. Since then, I have been thanking God for my husband's leaving and even for this other woman, but I haven't been able to feel the joy and

76

peacefulness that the Holy Spirit gives. I've committed this whole thing to God, and asked Him for my husband's salvation. My husband has always been such a good person, that he thinks he doesn't need God.

My Comments

When things are going well, we often do not realize our need of God. Your marriage and home may be holding together while you continue to do things you know you shouldn't, and leave undone things you know you should do. God in His goodness may pull the props out from everything that is holding you together and let you see how much you need Him. He loves you too much to permit life to run smoothly before praise has become a positive force in your life.

One person told me, "There is as much difference in my life since I learned to praise God for everything as there was when I was first filled with the Holy Spirit. Praise has completely changed my attitude toward life. I haven't experienced a moment of unrest since praise came into my life. Praise has given me more peace of mind than I ever had before."

Answer to Your Praise

Dear Sir,

This letter isn't an answer to my praise, but it sure is an answer to your praise. For ten years I did everything I could think of to help my husband accept Christ. I prayed, believed, fasted, and prayed some more. I left pieces of literature where I hoped he would read them, but he never did. I attended clinics on how to be a good wife and was as loving to my husband as I knew how to be.

My efforts helped us to get along great, but my husband seemed further from accepting Christ than ever. Then I heard how a wife had given *Prison to Praise* to her husband. It was the first Christian book he ever read. I decided to get a copy and try that. To my delight, my husband saw the book and started reading it. I literally held my breath while I prayed he would keep reading. He read the entire book before he got out of his chair! Even after he was through, I didn't say a word for fear I would disrupt whatever God was doing. The next day he said, "What do you think about that book?"

I said, "What book?"

"The one about the Army chaplain. Do you think those things really happened?"

We talked about the book for a long while, and he discovered that he had a new interest in finding out what it was to be a Christian. He soon accepted Christ and was then filled with the Holy Spirit. Thank you for praising the Lord!

My Comment

At the center of every man, there is a desire for praise. God built this desire into his creation. Man can mis-direct or mis-use the desire, but it is still an instinct created by God. When man hears or reads about praise to God, it touches the instinct within him even when he does not realize what is happening to him. This arouses an interest and often leads to his being released from the outward facade of unconcern.

If you cannot get someone to read a book on praise, you still have a powerful tool you can use. Simply live a life of praise. Being filled with a daily attitude of praise and joy will reach another person's heart even when they do not know what you are doing. If you are irritable, cross, and critical you push people away from God. If you are at peace, joyful, and considerate, they will be moved toward God. Don't expect instant results. People who have seen hundreds of professing Christians over many years demonstrating all the pitiful characteristics of non-Christians, will not immediately respond to your spirit of praise. (It may take a whole day.)

Born Damaged

Dear Reverend Carothers,

Your book *Power in Praise* is right on. I'm a junior in high school, and am really turned on for Christ. When I read your book about praising God for everything that has happened, I could hardly believe it. When I was born, I suffered brain damage that affected my ability to walk. I couldn't see how I could praise God for that. I sure hadn't in the past! I always wondered why God let me be born, if I had to be a cripple. Even after I was a Christian, I wished I hadn't been born.

When I tried doing what you said to do — boy, I couldn't believe what happened to me. I got so excited I could hardly stand it. When I thanked God for my problem, I started feeling like I was the luckiest person in the whole wide world. That was several months ago, and I'm still on cloud nine. I used to have to try and cheer myself up, but now I have to hold my laughter down. I feel so great I can hardly stand it! What has happened to me?

My Answer

You were carrying around the heavy burden of complaining against God. When you got rid of that by praising Him, you were relieved of a great hindrance. You are now free to grow in Christ. Continue to praise God for everything and He will give you many new joys. The best is yet to come!

My Comments

The burden of complaining is far greater than most people realize. Satan uses it to dump all kinds of sadness upon us. If there are times when you have a heavy heart, it can probably be traced to your complaining about something. You may feel your complaint is justified, but is it worth the sadness that clings to you? Is God unfair to want you filled with the same joy His Son had?

Reputation Attacked

Dear Brother in Christ,

I don't know how it started, but an ugly rumor was destroying my reputation. It was being spread all over my community, and the members of my congregation were hearing it everywhere.It was evident to me that they were thinking, "Where there is smoke, there must be fire." My church board asked me to meet with them and expressed their great concern over the things they were hearing about their pastor. The leaders of my denomination invited me to come and share with them the accusations being made about me.

The rumors were such that there seemed to be no way of pinning them down. No one seemed to know where they originated. For weeks I went through real hell. Daily and sometimes hourly, I gave it over to the Lord and promised I would trust Him to work it out. By the next day I was wrestling with the problem again. It seemed to me that if God was going to let the rumor persist, I should get out of the ministry for good, and yet I knew God had called me to preach. The more I tried to decide what to do, the more confused I became.

Then a dear brother brought me your two books, *Prison to Praise* and *Power in Praise*. He said, "If anyone ever needed these books, you do." Reading books didn't appeal to me at the time, but I agreed to look at them. After a few pages, my attention was so captured that I couldn't put the books down.

By the last page, I knew what had to be done. I couldn't merely accept the problem, I had to praise God for it. This, I confess, was a real battle for me, but God helped me, and I was able to honestly thank Him for everything exactly as it was. At that very moment, God spoke to me more clearly than I had ever heard Him speak before. He said, "You had to be broken that you might be of better service to Me. Now that you understand what it feels like, you are prepared to serve Me in a new way."

From that day on, miracles began to happen in my
ministry that I had never seen before. People were healed and
filled with the Holy Spirit in astounding ways. I could see
people's attitudes toward me changing. They seemed to be
saying, "God wouldn't use you as He is if those rumors were
true."

Praise the Lord for revealing through you the glorious
truth of praise.

My Comments

As painful as it may be, it is often necessary for God to
permit Satan to destroy even our reputation. Jesus became
"of no reputation" in order that He might suffer unjustly for
our sake. We should not be surprised when we are punctured
by arrows of accusation. Our human reasoning may insist
that an unspotted reputation would be far more effective
than one held in question, but God knows what He wants to
do with us. There are people He wants to reach who would
close their ears to anyone except the man or woman God is
making out of you. He loves those people and wants to reach
them regardless of what the cost may be. He permitted His
own Son to die a shameful death on a cross between two
thieves, and He will permit you and me to endure whatever
He knows will help others. Our praise and trust open wide
the door for Him to use us according to His own plan.

*The God of all grace, who hath called us unto his eternal
glory by Christ Jesus, after that ye have suffered a while,
make you perfect, stablish, strengthen, settle you. (I Pet.
5:10)*

My Wife Left Me

Dear Sir,

Since I read your books, I have been trying to thank God that my wife left me, but I can't do it. Every time I think about her, I can do nothing but cry. I'm getting less and less able to do my work, and I don't even care. I seldom eat a full meal, and I'm never hungry. How can I be thankful that I feel so terrible? I'm not able to help anyone else, and I would like to use my life for something worthwhile.

When my wife first left me, friends told me I would get over it with time. But time is making me worse. I love my wife, and the longer she is gone, the more I miss her. Shouldn't people who love someone be sad when they leave? There are many times that I do wrong, but I don't feel wrong about missing my wife. Do you think I am wrong? You help many people — can you help me?

My Answer

Yes, you are wrong, my friend. You are permitting Satan to destroy you. You believe your sorrow is "right," so you carefully hold on to it. When you realize that it is wrong, you will let go of it and God will give you a new life.

It is wrong to doubt God regardless of the circumstances. It may be natural not to want pain of any kind, just as it is natural not to want separation from someone we love. But even Jesus "learned obedience by the things which he suffered" (Heb. 5:8). If you want your situation to be used by God to bless you and others, begin to thank Him that your wife is gone. At first it may seem impossible, but do your best and God will honor that. He only requires you to do what you are able to do.

It isn't your wife's departure that is killing you, it is your own reaction to it. God permits you to react however you choose, but He will give you peace if you will thank Him that everything is exactly as it is and trust Him to work good out of it exactly as He promised. What good? Bring your wife back? Only He knows the good that needs to be done, and this must be left to Him.

I will be in prayer with you that the Holy Spirit will help you to believe that God is with you and has a perfect plan for you and your wife.

Dear Sir,

When I received your letter, my reaction was "You're nuts!" I kept on feeling sorry for myself. But your prayer must have gotten through! I went back and read *Power in Praise* again and decided to give praise a good try. At first I felt like a real hypocrite, but once I got started, I knew I had to either make it that time or I would never try it again. I kept on saying, "Thank You, God." After a while, I could tell that I was feeling a little bit better. When I was convinced that I was a little better, I got excited. God was actually doing something for me!

You were right. My self-pity gradually left. I saw that I needed God much more than I needed my wife. I still love her and want her, but I'm learning what it means to need God, too. He has a plan for my life, so I am going to enjoy finding out what it is. Several times lately, I've seen an opportunity to do something for someone else, and I actually enjoyed doing it. When I was crying like a baby, I thought only of myself. It is like I was in a fog and am now starting to see the sunshine. Please keep praying for me. God must have more things He wants to do in me.

My Comments

It will take a lifetime for God to complete His plan for our lives. When that plan is completed, we are then ready for heaven. In heaven we will be relieved of all our problems, but here on earth we need to experience whatever suffering will fit us for the eternal plan He has for us. You are being prepared to serve Him in your own special way for all eternity. God could have started your eternity in heaven with

83

the angels, but you were to come here first and learn whatever you needed to know. If you choose to grumble and fight against His will for you, you will be like the man who beats his head against a stone wall. That really isn't the purpose for a wall. Doubting God isn't the purpose for life either!

Polio

Dear Pastor Carothers,

I deeply appreciated your letter and am sorry I didn't acknowledge it sooner. I have read and re-read it many times. I had always thought I was a good Christian (Catholic), but until I read your books, I did not have the faith I have now. I have prayed to God for over fifty years, but I don't believe that I ever praised Him for my infirmities before (I had polio at the age of two). I know that polio made me a stronger person, as I have had to struggle for many things. God has blessed me in many ways and now I am thanking Him for my infirmity as well as asking Him to heal me.

I have been attending prayer meetings, and have discovered that by praying with others, I have come closer to God. Since your letter, I have the faith and the confidence that some day He will heal my leg. I feel it so strongly. At two of the prayer meetings, I felt His closeness, and for the first time I actually have had tears in my eyes. After my husband's death, leaving me with two young sons to rear, I withheld tears so long that I didn't think it was possible for them to start coming again. My work is more pleasant, too. I can overlook gossip, unpleasantness in the surroundings, and just praise Him.

Thank you for writing to me, and may God give you the strength to continue imparting faith to others.

My Comments

Tears have been "shut off" by some who have permitted grief to overcome them. Others in self-pity cry nearly continually. In either case, the sufferer is shutting off the peace of mind now enjoyed by the writer of this letter. The person guilty of self-pity often feels so completely justified in his sorrow that he highly resents anyone even hinting that his pain is self-imposed.

It is easier to blame suffering on others than it is to accept full responsibility and then permit God to do something about it. Problems caused by situations completely beyond your human control do not give you license to give in to the agony of self-pity. If you do so, you permit Satan to heap pain upon you that God does not intend for you to bear. If you will give up the temptation from Satan to drown yourself in self-pity, God will abundantly reward you.

Believe that His Son was telling you the truth when He promised to supply all of your needs. Your faith in Christ opens the door for God to do whatever needs to be done in you. The writer of this letter is being transformed by her trust in God. Instead of keeping her eyes on the physical problem, she has realized the good that God is working in her. Her spirit is being healed by God, and her joy is beginning to rise. She is being prepared for eternal life! With a sound physical body, her spirit might have had little interest in seeking God's will. Satan thought affliction would beat her down, but she has permitted her faith in God's goodness to actually cause the polio to work for her good. I praise the Lord for helping her to see the tremendous power there is in praise. I would not be surprised to hear that the polio has finished its usefulness and that she is being healed in body.

And ye shall serve the Lord your God . . . and I will take sickness away from the midst of thee. (Exod. 23:25)

85

A Short Journey

Dear Pastor Carothers,

I know there are many women who feel lonely even though they are married. But believe me, the divorced woman is the most desolate.

I'm aware that a widow is very lonely, yet her husband is "gone." When a woman is divorced, her husband is around, somewhere. He's alive and breathing, but not with his family. It doesn't matter, at this point, who filed for the divorce. The loneliness is devastating. But praise the Lord, it doesn't have to be devastating. I know. Precious Jesus. I am divorced. I've felt so alone, almost to the point of a mental breakdown. Now, I've found what I was looking for. I've found joy, peace — without resentment. Praise God! I've found out what real Christianity is.

What is it like, being divorced? A few months ago I would have said it's the most terrible, horrible feeling in the world. I'm not condoning divorce, but it does happen. And there you are with nothing — or so you think! It does not have to be that way. Praise the Lord! If anyone feels alone for any reason, please tell them about me. Especially if they are divorced. Beg them to listen. I have been divorced three years. In that time, I've reached the absolute bottom of despair. I've seen my ex-husband marry the woman who helped destroy our marriage, and my children have been given to them by the court because they could offer "a more stable home atmosphere with two parents in the home."

I was living in California during this part of my life. I called my mother in Florida one day and told her I thought I was cracking up. I was walking a tightrope, and I was about to fall off. She told me to pray. Well, I tried to pray. Nothing happened. Then one day, a large envelope came in the mail from Mom. Inside was a copy of *Prison to Praise* by Merlin Carothers. I read it and then re-read it. I called Mom.

"I'm just not too sure," I told her, "what I think about that book."

Then my mother sent me your book, *Power in Praise.*
Praise God. That finally got me started. I praised God for
everything I could think of — my divorce, the children being
with their daddy, everything. My whole attitude changed. A
friend of mine said to me, "What's happening with you?
There's such a glow on your face." And that was before I
received the Holy Spirit. Praise the Lord.

I went home to work for my father and began the most
wonderful journey of my life — to the Holy Spirit and Jesus.
One week after I arrived, I received the Baptism in the Holy
Spirit. And I spoke in tongues. I had been a chain smoker for
two years, smoking two packs a day. The night I received the
Baptism, I had the nicotine habit taken from me. I've not
wanted a cigarette since! Thank You, Jesus.

I've put the lives of my children in the Lord's hands. He
has heard me. I don't know how He is doing it, I don't
question it, I just know He is sending my children to me. In
the meantime, I praise Him for letting them be with their
daddy and his wife.

I feel at peace. I feel joy. I've seen miracles. My own dad,
for one. He's been healed of two gastric ulcers and a hiatal
hernia. Praise God. There is no need for anyone to worry or
feel alone. None whatsoever! They can trust Him, step out in
faith. Every sorrow and care will be gone. Hallelujah. The
journey from darkness into light is so short. Once it's been
made, the life left behind seems so long ago.

My Comment

A flick of a switch, and light floods a dark room. A sudden
realization that God will use every detail of every experience
in our life to bless us, and a light comes on. The despair of
inward darkness is gone, and the peace of God moves in.

Thank You, God, for providing this unfailing answer to
every problem. Please help us to share it with as many people
as possible.

And let us not be weary in well doing: for in due season we shall reap, if we faint not. (Gal. 6:9)

I Asked For The Baptism

Dear Reverend Carothers,

I have been asking for the Baptism in the Holy Spirit and have been aching to receive it. I am surprised to hear other people say they do not want to speak in tongues, for I would be glad to do this or anything else God wanted me to do. Others have prayed for me several times, but I have received nothing. My question is, "How can I possibly praise the Lord that I have not received what I know would help me to be a better witness for Christ?"

My Answer

I praise the Lord for your desire. Only the Holy Spirit could help you to want Christ's Baptism. Yes, I believe you should praise the Lord that you have not received it. I have several reasons, but even if I didn't have them, I would still believe that you were not receiving the blessing from God for some very good reason.

Many times people do not receive the Baptism in the Holy Spirit because they do not understand it. They seek an emotion or feeling, and this is definitely not what the Baptism is. If God gave you what you think Christ's Baptism should be instead of what it is, God would not be faithful to you. I therefore find it very easy to be thankful that you have not received it.

When you asked God to baptize you in the Holy Spirit, did you ask Him in Jesus' name? Did you come to Him on the basis of a promise His Son made to you? From what you write, I believe you did. What did you do next? You then told God, yourself, and others that Jesus' promise was not true. He said God would answer your prayer, and God "didn't do it." Someone was wrong — you or Jesus. I believe you were wrong and Jesus was right. When you asked God for the Baptism in the Holy Spirit, Jesus immediately responded to your prayer. But you disbelieved and fell back. The next time you ask God to let His Son baptize you, do not leave His presence and go out to deny His Son. Know that He has done what He promised.

If ye then . . . know how to give good gifts unto your children: how much more shall your heavenly Father give the Holy Spirit to them that ask him? (Luke 11:13)

My Comments

Many people are confused about what the Baptism in the Holy Spirit is and are guilty of disbelieving Christ's promises. In Luke 11:13, Jesus promised that God would give to those who ask Him. This is a simple straightforward promise that many people have tried to complicate. Jesus meant it when He said, "Ask with your heart, and God will give."

"But I haven't spoken in tongues yet," many have told me. "Isn't speaking in tongues one of the signs I should receive?" Yes, this is correct if the emphasis is placed on the word "should." Your lack of faith could hold back the sign, but this does not nullify Christ's promise. When you have earnestly asked God to baptize you in the Holy Spirit, believe that He has. Believe that all the gifts and fruit of the Spirit are dwelling within you and will be made manifest according to your faith. If someone asks, "Have you received the Baptism?" your answer should be, "Yes, I have!" This is a step of faith that God will surely honor. Thank Him for what He has done, and then praise Him. Let your praise be in your heart and on your lips.

If someone asks you, "Have you received a new language?" your answer should be a strong positive "Yes." This is merely confirming what Jesus said: "And these signs shall follow them that believe; . . . they shall speak with new tongues" (Mark 16:17). We are not supposed to require evidence before we believe His promise. Rejoice in your heart, and know that God has given you through His Spirit the new language He wants you to have, plus the freedom to use all the gifts of the Spirit as the need arises.

What should you say if someone asks you at this point, "Have you ever prayed in tongues?" You should give a firm unembarrassed, "No, I haven't used my new prayer language yet, but God has given it to me."

God always honors this kind of faith. Keep your heart and mind open to listen to His Spirit within you. You will soon hear words that do not, at first, mean anything to you. Open your mouth and speak them. Your first utterance may cause you to explode in joy, or you may feel nothing. You are being obedient to Christ, and He will take care of the feelings in His own time. He wants you first to grow in faith. The Baptism in the Holy Spirit was designed by God to help you grow in faith. Satan may whisper to you, "You only made those words up in your own mind." Quickly give your mind to God and tell Him, "Father, You have my mind, and I want You to use it for Your glory."

Then proceed to let the Holy Spirit use your tongue to talk to God. You may have one word, or many. The numbers are unimportant. Your faith in Christ is what is important. It was through faith in Christ that you received eternal life. It is through faith in Christ that God gives you His Baptism in the Holy Spirit.

When Abraham believed in Him, God promised to use him to build a mighty nation. God's plan has always been for man to believe Him. Whenever He finds a man or woman who will believe, He pours out His blessings upon them. Speaking in tongues is a result of your faith in God. You believe, and God gives you all the feeling, power, gifts, and fruit of the Spirit that you can possibly contain. He does not give sparingly or grudgingly, but He can give only to those who will believe and trust Him.

If you have been honestly seeking the Baptism in the Holy Spirit, and you know that Christ is your Savior, you can at this moment believe that His promise is fulfilled in you. Do not doubt for any reason, and soon "rivers of living water" will be flowing from within you.

Jesus stood and cried, saying, If any man thirst, let him come unto me, and drink. He that believeth on me, as the scripture hath said, out of his belly shall flow rivers of living water. (But this spake he of the Spirit, which they that believe on him should receive .... (John 7:37-39)

He Can Do It For Anybody

Dear Pastor Carothers,

In 1970, sometime toward the end of the year, my pastor played your tape from a FGBMFI meeting. Later a friend had the tape, and I listened to it again, but since my problems at the time were so enormous, I had little understanding.

A few weeks after my husband left me with a three-year-old and seven-week-old baby, I was told of your book. A friend offered to take me to the bookstore that day, and I bought the last copy of *Prison to Praise.* I read it through in a few hours. For the next three days, even with tears and an aching heart, I praised God. Nothing happened until the night of the third day. While I was talking about God, something inside me broke, and I began to bubble, then laugh and laugh. This lasted for three days, and when I "came down," it was to normal, not the horrible depression I had before.

Then, through the horrible nightmarish days that followed, I tried to keep praising God and giving thanks in obedience to His Word. I had put so many barriers up that God had to pull them down to get through to me. Having been absolutely broken, I nearly lost my mind, but God was holding on to it. Then I set my mind to eat His Word. As often as I had coffee, I read His Word, mainly the Psalms. I saw that no matter how David felt, or what was going on, he ended up praising God. As I praised, I was filled with joy — His joy. The joy healed my mind. I was 100 percent better after the first week.

About six weeks later, I bought *Power in Praise,* and was thrilled that you were teaching about some of the things God had taught me. God gave me understanding as to what He had done in my life — and why. I thought my world had come to an end when my husband turned his back on God; now I have hope and the ability to let God work. Nothing can happen to the three of us without God's allowing it. And whatever happens will bring glory to Him, and blessing to us.

I don't know if you can appreciate to the fullest what God has done, because it's hard to tell how bad life was for me. I gave up many times and twice tried suicide. Certainly it was the Holy Spirit that protected and sustained me. Because I've survived through so many problems, I can understand others, and tell them I know praising God works. I've done it — rather, God's done it in me for His glory.

Recently I found I had to make myself swallow tears and say, "Praise the Lord!" Just last Friday I arrived at work and found I no longer had a job. I said, "Praise the Lord!" It was my first thought and response. That's what God has done for me. I know if God can make a happy Christian out of me, He can do it for anybody.

My Comments

No sudden change in the situation, nothing radical. Just a growing assurance that God is watching over us. This is the best result we can have in praising God! Most people are excited about the abrupt transforming power of praise. It excites me, too, but I'm even more excited over the possibility of growing in solid faith in God. This faith demands no outward manifestation of God's power. It says, "God I trust You whether You change my situation or not." Rejoice if you have learned that God trusts you to trust Him!

Him that cometh to me I will in no wise cast out. (John 6:37)

Eyes Off Problem

Dear Chaplain Carothers,

We find ourselves in dire financial difficulty. It is hard for us, faced with more bills than we can pay, to keep our eyes off our problems and upon Christ.

I have promised the Lord that I will praise Him in all things if He will teach me how. I do realize already that He has permitted our difficulty to bring us into a closer walk with Him.

Since we have brought many of our problems upon ourselves, it is a relief to know that God is in charge and that He has permitted all of them for our good and His Glory. It removes the burden of guilt, which kept coming back even though we had confessed our sins and knew we were forgiven.

Please pray for us that we will remain constant in praise and thanksgiving, no matter what. We do accept the fact that it is the will of God for us to give thanks in everything. Once you see it, there's no getting around it!

My Comments

The temptation to keep our eyes on the problem rather than on praising God is often overpowering. As a result, we become part of the problem rather than of the solution.

One mother's son commits suicide, and she spends the rest of her life in fear and agony. Another mother believes that God in His great goodness understands and forgives and keeps on loving. Someone might tell her "Impossible," but she knows that in Christ *all things* are possible. She lives in the midst of the peace that passes all understanding.

Foundation of Praise

Dear Reverend Carothers,

In your book you write about giving your books to men in prison. I would like to have a part in work like that. Please let me know how much you need at this time, and I will do my best to help.

My Answer

Thank you for wanting to help. All of my own personal needs have already been abundantly met by God. The need for books to give men in prison is absolutely unlimited. If I had one million dollars to use to supply books to prisoners, the project would only be started! Few people realize how many men are behind bars.

To supply books for hospitals and servicemen would require many more millions of dollars. We are, however, not responsible for what we cannot do. God asks us only to do what we can. I know that for the price of one book, many prisoners have accepted Christ as Savior and are now daily doing their best to lead other men to Christ.

God will take your best and multiply it many times over. Please ask Him what you should do.

An Army General

Dear Chaplain,

Nearly all of my adult life has been spent in trying to make the Army the professional and effective force I believe it should be. I advanced steadily in rank, for God gave me a good mind and an ability to concentrate on details.

I woke up one day to realize that my dedication to the Army had cost me far more than I realized. My wife no longer cared anything for me. My two sons resented everything I said or did. My wife's poodle was the only member of the family who seemed to care anything about me. I responded with bitterness and self-pity, and things got even worse.

Our post chaplain brought me your book, *Prison to Praise,* and urged me to read it. I promised him I would, just to get him off my back. I didn't know what I was getting into! Your life and ideas really hit me in in the pit of my stomach. I realized that there was something to religion that I had never known anything about. I never would have tried your ideas on praising God if it hadn't been for the fantastic stories you told in the first part of your book. I decided you either had to be a big liar or the discoverer of something I needed.

I started thanking God for my life and home as it was. To my absolute amazement, one of my sons came in that night and said, "Hi, Dad. How are things?" That might sound very trivial to some people, but to me it was a signpost. I kept thanking God. Things kept happening right and left — things I could hardly believe.

I know you must receive thousands of letters, but I wanted to tell you that as a result of praising God, my entire life has changed. I have a family now. We love one another and enjoy life together. I'm seeking God's will in many ways.

I'm very proud to share your books with others, and I've urged the post chaplain to get as many as he can.

My Comments

God is moving in every area of American life. Men at every level of our society are being drawn to Him. It may come as a surprise to some of you former military personnel that God loves generals, too!

A lifetime of mistaken priorities can ring the death knell on what should be a happy family. No amount of self-incrimination can change what has already been done. But God has the sovereign power to overcome the most awful mistakes when we praise Him. Men who have solved the most complex problems in their profession are often stymied in efforts to get out of the prison of unhappiness in their homes. God alone holds the answer to this problem, and He has revealed it to us through Christ.

In Prison

Dear Chaplain Carothers,

I am an inmate in a prison, and I have just finished reading *Prison to Praise*. I felt the power of God as I read what He did in your life.

I really thank God for guiding you to write such a Spirit-filled book. It has changed me so that I am able to accept my own life. I never thought I could be glad to be where I am, but now I can honestly say, "Praise You, Lord, for getting me into prison!" I know it was the Lord's will to bring me here. I know He has a work for me to do, and I am thankful that He arranged whatever was necessary to get me started.

Merlin Carothers, I wonder how I would have been had I met you when I was in the Army. When I was in Vietnam, I became addicted to dope. When I came back, I was given an undesirable discharge. From there, I went into armed robbery to support my habit. Praise God, I got arrested and sentenced to a four-year minimum term in prison. Soon after my arrival here, another prisoner led me to accept Christ. I have found a real happiness and joy in Jesus Christ as Lord. Never again will I be lonely or feel unloved.

I really praise God for the blessings He has bestowed upon all His children. Please include me in your prayers, and always thank God that I am here, for here I received eternal life. Whenever Satan decides to give me a rough time, I remind him that it was within these stone walls that I was delivered from his prison. The guards cannot understand why I am so filled with joy. Frequently I see them looking at me as if they wonder what has happened to me. Whenever I get the opportunity, I tell them that Jesus has happened to me.

My Comments

Do you believe that God can change whatever "prison" Satan has built around you into a place of joy? The more difficult your situation happens to be, the more powerful will be the change that God will work in you through His Son, Jesus. Any self-pity that you may feel, for whatever reason, is a testimony to Satan that you do not believe that Jesus Christ came into this world to set you free from all bondage. In wartime, this is called "giving comfort to the enemy."

Where the Spirit of the Lord is, there is liberty. (II Cor. 3:17)

My Appetite

Dear Reverend Carothers,

I guess my husband is a compulsive drinker. He drinks to feel good, to forget his problems. I keep telling him that God will solve our problems if he will just quit drinking, but I can't get through to him. I hate drinking and I know it isn't God's will. Please pray that he will quit.

I know that the Holy Spirit has given me leadership in many things and has given me understanding of His Word. I want nothing in my life that is of self or sinful. I want to honor God in every way possible.

One thing I have not been able to overcome is my appetite. I am unable to control it. I gain more and more weight and I know this does not please God, but what can I do?

My Comments

Millions of people are asking God to control appetites of one kind or another that have become their prisons. If you have this problem, let me share a very powerful secret with you. Your appetite may indeed be so strong that you cannot make it go away. But there is one thing you do have the power to do! Stop gratifying the appetite!

"But I feel so bad if I don't gratify my appetite," you say. So what? Go ahead and feel bad. God will not heal your appetite while you are doing everything you can to make it worse. He will heal the appetite if you will let go of it long enough for Him to make it well.

This woman sees her own appetite for food as uncontrollable but her husband's appetite for drink as controllable. Both problems come from the individual's unwillingness to do what God has given us the power to do. When we do our part, He will take care of the part we can do nothing about.

The glorious thing is that God loves us whether we do our part or not. If we want to grow fat and die of overweight, He will forgive us. Thank God, He provides the answers to our needs but doesn't condemn us if we are too weak to accept His answers.

Do you have an appetite for something you know is hurting you? You can — right now through Christ — stop satisfying it long enough for God to heal you. How long does it take? As long as it takes for you to believe He has done it!

For the kingdom of God is not meat and drink; but righteousness, and peace, and joy in the Holy Ghost. (Rom. 14-17)

A Point of Contact

Dear Brother Carothers,

My, what a bombshell your books have been to us! It seems like everything is embodied in praise. The Holy Spirit is surely using it to speak to people. The way people are catching hold of praise proves that these must be the last days in which the Lord is drawing in all He can before the end. The Baptism in the Holy Spirit is sweeping along with it. Though I worship in a fundamental Bible church where I know they do not accept the Baptism as something for today, I plan to put your books in the church library. Praise and thank the Lord with me for what He will do.

I discovered in reading *Answers to Praise* several testimonies that fitted me. I decided instead of just "reading and enjoying" the book that I should make each letter or teaching in it a point of contact, drawing me closer to God. As I did, I found nearly every one had something of value for my life.

I've only one sad note. The friend's book I first read had your picture on the back, and these I've ordered do not have. I realize the message is more important than the channel it goes through, but that shining smile confirms the book. I wish the smile could be on every copy.

My Comments

Many people have written me saying, "I have read your first three books and enjoyed them very much." They then go into great detail in explaining their own problem and urge me to pray for them. I do pray for everyone who writes, and my prayer is always the same: "Thank You, Lord, for this situation and the glorious victory You are going to win because of it."

How beautifully refreshing it is to see that this reader has listened to what God has taught others and has used their

99

experiences to strengthen her own life. We might just as well profit from the mistakes of others, for we aren't going to live long enough to make them all ourselves!

Now all these things happened unto them for ensamples: and they are written for our admonition. (I Cor. 10:11)

Suicide

Dear Chaplain Carothers,

I went to a hotel and rented a room with one purpose in mind. I wanted a private place to take my life. When the bell boy left, I started my preparations. I sat at a desk to write my farewell letter to the world I hated so much.

On the desk was a bright colored book that caught my eyes, *Prison to Praise.* I had been in prison, so I picked it up to see what another poor soul might have been through in the world. As I read your story, my eyes filled with tears, and I couldn't put it down.

Your story did something to me that I thought would never happen. It made me believe there was a God!

Lying on the floor and asking God to do something for me, I heard a voice that said, "Look for a Bible." I got up and found one there in the room. On the first page I opened to, I saw "You must be born again." I didn't know what it meant, but I asked God to do that for me, and something happened inside. I began to laugh like I never had laughed before in all my life.

Suddenly I was so happy I wanted to tell the whole world what God had done for me. I went down to the lobby and tried to tell someone. Everyone acted as if they thought I was drunk. I went back to my room and read the Bible all night. I didn't know it was such a great Book.

Thank you for writing your book. It saved my life. Or rather, it gave me a new one. Now I can even praise God for the old one.

My Comments

I know, and most of you know, that the Bible is God's Holy Word. But it isn't much use to tell this to 95 percent of the people in our country. If they don't believe you, they will not read it. If they believe you, they might say "So what?" and still never read it.

We need to get books into peoples' hands that will help them to believe that the Bible has the answer to their needs! I may never know who placed that copy of *Prison to Praise* in a hotel room, but whoever you are, "Thank you." Does anyone else know of a hotel, motel, prison, hospital, or military post where there are people who need to be "turned on" to the Bible and set free from their prison?

A Prison Guard

Dear Sir,

I've asked myself a thousand times why I ever decided to become a prison guard. I believe it is the hardest job a man could have. For eleven years I wondered each day I came to work if that would be the day I would get a knife in my back.

I think everyone likes to work in a pleasant place, but this place was anything but pleasant. We've been overcrowded and poorly equipped for as long as I have been here. The men have always been angry and seemed to be on the edge of riot all the time. We've had to be on constant alert, and I usually went home dead tired. I took my weariness and frustrations and fears out on my family, and even home was bad — like another prison.

Then, suddenly, I noticed that one of the prisoners had a complete change of attitude. He was getting his food one day when I saw him smile and say, "Praise the Lord." The food was especially bad that day, and I wondered what he was up to. I watched him carefully to see what he might do next. As he ate, he kept on smiling as if he knew something good was going to happen. Naturally this worried me, so I told the other guards to be on their toes.

This went on for several days, and then I heard another man saying, "Praise the Lord," when he was assigned a job none of the men like. My curiosity got the better of me, and I asked him, "Why did you say that?"

He said, "I read a book that Joe has, and I'm feeling better all the time."

Joe was the man I had noticed first. I went to him and asked to see the book. It was *Prison to Praise*. I looked to see if it had been approved by the librarian. He had signed it, all right.

When my curiosity couldn't stand it any longer, I asked Joe to let me read his book. It had been read so much the pages were held together with adhesive tape, but I got the message. From that time on, I've noticed a continuing change in this entire block. More and more men come to work singing. They laugh and joke. I come to work feeling good and go home feeling even better.

If you can spare some more copies of *Prison to Praise* I will be glad to share them with other parts of this prison. The chaplain says he isn't supposed to solicit anything for free, but no one has told me I can't do it.

God bless you. If you are helping others like you have helped me and the men here, please keep it up. I've been going to church all my life, but I've never believed in God like I do now.

My Comments

There are very few correctional institutions in our country that have happy people in them. Overcrowding, insufficient staff, and unhealthy living conditions are common. But the heart of the problem is men and women without hope of ever finding anything better. Nearly every man was unhappy when he went in, and in spite of his most optimistic dreams, he knows that life will be even tougher when he gets out. What incentive does he have to do better? Usually none. His only hope is that someone will introduce him to Jesus. "Religion" may be a dirty word to him, but he will respond to the love of Jesus. Anything we can do to reach into his heart with the good news of the Gospel will be rewarded.

Recently I sent a large supply of *Prison to Praise* to this guard. He has since told me that there is a spiritual move in his prison more powerful than anything he has seen on the outside.

I Began to Search

Dear Mr. Carothers,

Six months ago, as our marriage began to go on the rocks, I started searching for God's will in our home. My husband, our seven-year-old daughter, and I were at a major crossroad in our lives. I had found out there was another woman in my husband's life. I was floored. I had never expected such a thing to happen to us. I thought we were so devoted to each other. Our friends were also flabbergasted. Our marriage had seemed the most perfect in our crowd.

I did my best to get my husband to stay with me, but he refused, claiming that he loved the other woman. When he moved in with her, I just tried, in my weakness, to trust the Lord. It wasn't easy.

They had been living together for over a week when your book, *Power in Praise,* was put in my hand. I had read only a few pages when I was moved to throw myself on the Lord, praising Him for all of this in my life. I thanked Him for time to read and study and grow. I thanked Him for the other woman. I thanked Him that my husband had left me. The Holy Spirit really rained down on me, overwhelming me, and I felt as if I was speaking in a new language.

I kept on searching for God's will for my life. I filed for divorce, and the papers were served on my husband on Tuesday night of this week. I never expected to see him again, as I knew his anger toward me would be terrible. But the next day he came to see me. We really talked, and he told me many things I had been doing for years that irked him. I began to see God telling me many things.

Now my husband wants to come home! Praise the God who loves us!

I have lots of doubts and fears, in a way. But I know that God can and will work everything out for our good. The battle is God's, not mine, and He knows best. I know that He is going to show us great and mighty things. I stand expectantly upon the promise He gave me in Jeremiah 33:3. "Call unto me, and I will . . . shew thee great and mighty things." I do praise God for everything.

My Comments

What will the outcome be? The important thing is that one more child of God has made a step toward trusting *Him* rather than conditions. Think of the power there is in faith in God — eternal life, His gifts, fruit of the Spirit. . . . Is it any wonder that God permits events in our lives that will help us to learn to trust Him? There is nothing like adversity to force us to learn what it means to trust God! He knows this, and whether you and I understand or not, He will permit Satan to stir up whatever trouble is necessary to build our faith. When adversity is raging, the human being often thinks, "If God would solve this problem, I really would trust Him." But this wouldn't be faith. Faith is not based upon evidence, but on things that are "not seen."

Faith is the substance of things hoped for, the evidence of things not seen. (Heb. 11:1)

Happy In Prison

Dear Merlin Carothers,

The chaplain here at Los Angeles County Jail gave me your books, *Prison to Praise* and *Power in Praise.* I read them on July 9, 1972. On that day I invited Jesus Christ to come into my heart and life as "my personal Savior." Anyhow, I heard those words somewhere, and they sound like what happened to me. Jesus is personal to me now. I know He saves me from my sins.

On the same day, I had here in my cell what you call the Baptism in the Holy Spirit. It was as if my mind had become alive again. I'm free in Christ. God has set me free in jail! On the outside, I was always in prison. I'm only twenty-one, but it seems as if I have been in prison somewhere for a hundred years. I was always mad at someone for making life so miserable for me. Now I know it wasn't people who were making me miserable, it was the devil, and I didn't even believe in Him!

Unless God changes things, I'll be in behind bars for a long while, but don't feel sorry for me. I'm the happiest I've been in all my life. For the first time I'm actually glad to be alive. The cop who busted me would never believe what a favor he did for me!

There are many unhappy people here, and I'm trying to help them. I'll be moving to a new place soon, and I know God will make it the right place. Pray that my coming days will help others to be thankful and to know our Savior.

My Comments

When I begin a new day, I often think of the men behind bars who are praying for an opportunity to tell someone about Jesus that day. Their freedom is very limited, and they must be ready to give a few words of the "Good News" when the opportunity comes. When that moment passes, the fellow prisoner will move on to his own private prison. If you have unlimited opportunities to move about and share Christ with others, please pray that God will give you lips that will quickly respond to every door God opens for you.

Preach the word; be instant in season, out of season . . . for the time will come when they will not endure sound doctrine. (II Tim. 4:2-3)

Crying in Prison

Dear Chaplain,

I hope you get this letter. I read your *Prison to Praise*, and I am in jail. I will be going to prison after my trial, for I'm guilty and will admit it. I know I have to pay for what I did, but I know the Lord will help me do it the best way possible.

I feel strange after writing that last sentence. I've never written or spoken about the Lord before, and I can hardly believe it's me writing!

Christians were a big nothing to me before I came here. Their big churches and fancy clothes turned me off. I didn't have anything decent, and couldn't understand why I was always so poor. I was mad about a lot of other things, too.

Then the man in the cell next to me handed me a book a few days ago and said, "You need this more than I did." When I saw it was something about religion, I didn't want to read it, but I didn't have anything else to read. The more I read it, the crazier I felt. I can't remember when I ever cried before that, but I sure made up for lost time. I wasn't unhappy, either.

You had been like me. You had found a way out. I started knowing I could, too. What a feeling that was! I had hope for the first time that life could be better for me.

While I was reading *Prison to Praise,* the fellow who gave it to me hollered, "What do you think of it?" I couldn't answer him right away, because I didn't want him to know I had been crying. But when I didn't answer, he guessed why. "Are you crying, too?" he asked me.

I was able to get out, "What do you mean?"

He said, "I know; I cried the whole way through it."

After I finished the book, we talked about our past lives, and then he said, "Could we do it too?"

"Do what?"

"Become churchgoers."

"No," I said, "that isn't for me. I don't want to be a churchgoer." Then he said he didn't want to either, but he wanted to be different than he had been. We talked until we agreed that what we wanted was to become Christian. I don't know if *we* did anything right or not, but something really happened to us. I *know* I'm a Christian now. I'm glad I came to jail! I'm glad for all the things that happened to you, sir, and glad for everything that brought me here.

If you have more books, please send them to me. I'll share them with the fellow in the next cell. He still has a lot of problems, but we keep saying, "Praise the Lord," and he hasn't complained once since we believed in God and Jesus.

My Answer

Yes, more books are on the way. People all over the United States are providing them for you, and other men like you. I'm pleased that you didn't decide to become just a "churchgoer." You have found Jesus, and that is far more important. Wherever you go in prison, there will be many unhappy men whom you can help. You belong to God now, and He will be with you every minute.

I'm sending you books about the Holy Spirit, also. The joy you have now will be greatly increased as you trust Jesus to baptize you in His Holy Spirit. You and your friends are in our prayers.

Humble yourselves therefore under the mighty hand of God, that he may exalt you in due time. (I Pet. 5:6)

107

Please Stay Humble

Dear Brother in Christ,

As a teacher of young married ladies, I am always seeking ways of growing in "grace and knowledge" that I might help them do likewise. (I'm a firm believer that you cannot teach what you do not know and cannot lead where you will not go.) Therefore, I look for books and helps of all kinds, and have Christian friends with whom I exchange these books. This is how I came to read *Prison to Praise* and *Power in Praise*. How they have changed my life!

The first time reading left me a bit doubtful, the second reading more interested. But by the third time around, I'm convinced. I am now giving your books to others. I have never written to any author before, but felt the Lord wanted me to tell you what a blessing your books have been to me and others. After reading *Answers to Praise*, I felt a real need to pray for you that you would stay humble and give all the glory to God. Maybe the thought was unmerited. How easy it would be for you to get puffed up with vainglory from people thanking you and praising you for all your wonderful help. May you continue to be used of the Lord as His servant as long as you live.

My Comments

I am very thankful for those who pray that God will keep me humble. I tremble at the thought of my even *thinking* that I am anything important. Without a doubt, I know that I am the least deserving of all God has ever called to do His will.

But I am not always praised. One woman wrote, "I can tell by the way you write that you are extremely proud of yourself."

"Thank You, Lord!"

I Was Searching

Dear Reverend Carothers,

I am the wife of an alcoholic who is a retired Army man. I accepted Christ as a teenager but drifted away through the years. My husband was not a Christian, and it was very easy for me to join the crowd with him. After his retirement, the drinking became worse, and I knew I must get back to God to keep my sanity. My father was a Methodist minister, and I knew wherein my source of strength was, but it has not been easy.

For over two years, I have struggled to regain the feeling of complete forgiveness that I knew when I accepted Christ as a teenager. I went to church faithfully, went to the altar many times, and prayed and was prayed for by my minister. I joined a special sharing group our minister organized and received a lot of peace, but every time my husband would go on a drinking bout, I became depressed and filled with all sorts of evil thoughts and emotions – anger, panic, hate, and fear. I could not feel a closeness to God and seemed to be still searching for fulfillment of some kind.

One morning a couple of weeks ago, I told my minister how I felt, and he handed me your book *Prison to Praise*. He had told me not to read it too fast, but I could not put it down and finished it before I went to sleep that night. Somewhere in the middle of the book, I was so moved that I got out of bed and fell to my knees and just poured out my soul to God and praised Him for my life as it is. I realized that what He had let happen in my life had brought me back to Him. An indescribable peace and joy came over me that I have never known before. The next day was Sunday, and I was so full of joy and love at church. I am praising God for my husband for his affliction and asking God to open his eyes to the Truth.

My Comments

"Thank you, pastor, for sharing *Prison to Praise*. Thank You, God, for helping this wife to believe." If you want God to do things for you, please *do not* try to hinge your faith on what He does for you. I know of no quicker way to stop God from working in your life than for you to insist you will believe *after* He does what you want.

What things soever ye desire, when ye pray, believe that ye receive them, and ye shall have them. (Mark 11:24)

My Minister

Dear Chaplain,

I gave a copy of *Prison to Praise* to our minister. When I asked him if he had read it, he said, "Yes, it was a good book. But do you believe in praying in tongues?"

"Yes, I do."

"Please do not distribute that book around the church," he said quite sternly.

"Why?" I asked.

"I believe speaking in tongues is of the devil and I do not want our people reading anything that will make them interested in it."

I was quite taken aback, and at first was real angry. Did he think I was going to contaminate the church? Then I realized that by getting angry I was playing into the devil's hands. I thanked the Lord that my minister was exactly as he was, and I believed God would do whatever needed to be done to win him to being filled with the Holy Spirit.

I asked several others in our church with whom I had shared your book to meet with me. We agreed to keep praising the Lord for our minister, to help him in every way we could, and to believe God would do something great.

Then an amazing thing happened. The richest and best-loved man of our church received a copy of *Prison to Praise* from his son. He went to the pastor to ask him to read it. When the pastor expressed strong misgivings about the book, he said, "Let's get his other books and see what we think of them." The pastor agreed, and they both read your *Power in Praise* and *Answers to Praise*. The man then contacted me and asked me what I thought of them.

Praise the Lord, I told him how much I loved praising the Lord and how richly God had blessed me since I received the Baptism in the Holy Spirit. I invited him to attend some of our weekly meetings to see what the Lord was doing. Again he went to the pastor and said, "I want to see what is going on within our church. Please go to one of these meetings with me so we can see for ourselves." To our delight, the pastor agreed to come!

You probably know what happened! He came once and then he came back again! He said later he only wanted to keep coming to try and learn what we were doing wrong! But before long, he asked us to pray for him, and he was baptized in the Holy Spirit! I had never seen him really laugh, but he laughed so long when he received the Baptism that I thought he would never stop.

My Comments

There is a story about a man who stood on the bank of a stream laughing at people who were in swimming. He got so close, he slipped and fell in!

Thank the Lord for laymen who have learned enough not to get upset with their minister. This never does any good. Thanking God will do something worthwhile. Of course, your praise to God may push him into the stream, but isn't that what you want?

Let not your heart be troubled: ye believe in God, believe also in me. (John 14:1)

111

I Was an Alcoholic

Dear Brother Merlin,

My life was one continuous tangle of drunkenness. I had been in all the jails and hospitals for alcoholics in the Atlanta area. I had a very obvious suicidal complex, and my psychiatrist predicted I would jump out of a hotel window. He told my family to write me off as a lost cause, and he refused to see me again, since I was drunk every time I went to his office.

Then on a cold sleety Sunday afternoon in March, 1948, a dear saint with a compassionate heart began witnessing to me about Jesus. My teeth were chattering with the cold, and I was about to shrug him off when he took off his coat, put it around my shoulders, and continued to claim me for Jesus. That impressed me, and I started to pay attention to what he was saying.

Praise God, He who would not let me go. I had already had my throat cut and been stabbed and cut many times. I strongly believe this was my last chance for salvation. On that day, God gave me complete victory over alcohol, and life has been wonderful ever since.

Last October I was loaned a copy of your *Prison to Praise*. (I've bought many copies since then.) Then followed a deep hunger for the Baptism in the Holy Spirit. I read and studied and prayed night and day. When nothing seemed to happen, I carried my Bible to my cabin in the mountains of north Georgia and determined to receive the Baptism or die. I had taught an adult Sunday school class for twenty-three years, but I was totally ignorant of the part faith plays in the reception of the Holy Spirit. In my cabin on Blood Mountain, God revealed the Truth to me, and by faith, I received the Baptism in the Holy Spirit and entered a new dimension of Life.

If ye shall ask any thing in my name, I will do it. (John 14:14)

My Comments

Since God inhabits the praises of His people, it is very natural for praise to bring a hungering for more of His Spirit. Redeemed alcoholics and men with every known infirmity are being drawn to His Spirit as they praise God. Little children are coming alive in Christ as parents teach them to praise God instead of grumbling and complaining. Very small children are developing a hunger for the Holy Spirit as they learn to step into God's "dwelling place." If children hear you grumble, you are literally encouraging them to step outside of God's home. If you happen to be grumbling about them, this does not lessen the harmful effect!

Overweight

Dear Reverend Carothers,

I have one problem that I can't get the victory over. I have been overweight for about as long as I have been saved. I always thought I could lose weight anytime I wanted to. But I was mistaken. I have been to doctors, taken diet pills, joined clubs, gone on all kinds of diets, and spent lots and lots of money to solve my problem — only to keep gaining more and more. My conscience bothers me when I eat things I know I shouldn't eat. I try to diet and I cannot.

I really need a miracle from God for the answer. I have thought maybe I'm supposed to be fat, but I do not feel well at all. I'm short of breath, and do not have enough energy to get my work done. It is not good for my heart, among other things, so I'm sure the Lord does not intend for it to be this way. My husband does not like it either.

I'm asking you to pray for me, and believe with me that the Lord will teach, show, lead, guide, or direct me in this matter. I'm not at all happy about my weight. I think about it all the time, and worry about it continually.

My Answer

Be sure of one thing — God loves you exactly as you are. This is very important for you to understand.

You ask for my help. Are you ready to receive advice? It may be hard to receive. Very often I receive letters from wives that read like this, "My husband has always been a strong moral man and a perfect father. He is the last man in the world that I would expect to be unfaithful. But I have just learned that he has been having an affair with another woman, and wants a divorce."

In many of these cases, the wife reports that the only problem they had was her overweight. She believed she was incapable of controlling her appetite for food, yet at the same time believed her husband should be able to control his appetite to have an attractive appealing wife.

You have the freedom to decide what you want most — to satisfy the desire to eat, or to satisfy the desire to have health and a happy home and family.

A decision of this kind will be extremely difficult for you to make. You need the help that Jesus wants to give you. He died to carry all your "grief." Ask Him to heal you of your excess appetite and believe that He has done it. If you experience symptoms that you are not completely healed, praise God. Rejoice that you are exactly as you are. I believe He is using even your appetite to draw you to Himself.

One woman who was having a terrible struggle with overeating wrote, "I didn't see how praising God could help me stop eating, but I followed your advice and kept praising Him, regardless of how I felt. In the midst of an especially difficult time, I received an infilling of joy that caused me to laugh and laugh. When this was over, I knew God had met a great need within me. I was well! The excessive desire to eat was gone and has stayed gone!"

114

My Comments

Yes, God is able to perform a miracle, and take away even our appetites, but He does not always do this. Often our choice must be made between enjoying one thing or another. Gratifying unhealthy desires, for whatever reason, nearly always results in our losing something that we really want much more. The freedom of choice that God gives us requires us to select the pleasures we really want. His love for us never changes, but when we make the wrong choice, we may have to endure unnecessary suffering.

God Uses Books

Dear Mr. Carothers,
I sent your books to my daughter-in-law. She started reading *Power in Praise,* got up the next Sunday, and went to church. She hadn't gone for almost a year. God filled her with the Holy Spirit, and she is teaching Sunday school now. She is believing God to save her husband and children.

My Comments

Praise the Lord for the way He is using books in this day. A greater percentage of people are reading Christian books now than at any previous time in history. God has truly put His hand upon the writing, publishing, and distributing of books He wants men to read. I'm thankful to have a very small part in what He is doing.

But these are written, that ye might believe that Jesus is the Christ, the Son of God; and that believing ye might have life through his name. (John 20:31)

115

Fear for Children

Dear Reverend Carothers,

It was through a divorce that I experienced salvation, my first encounter with Christ. Then fifteen years later, one of my sons was sent to prison. It was through this most painful experience that I received the Baptism in the Holy Spirit. God used another son and his alcoholism to bring me to understand God as my Father. God used still another son, my youngest, and his involvement with drugs to deliver me from a sick fear about my children and the terrible things they were doing.

I had this fear deep within me, in my mind, and grief in my Spirit. I knew I was saved, and had the Baptism in the Holy Spirit, yet I had this awful fear that was nearly destroying my life.

After I read your book, *Power in Praise,* it set me to thinking. For the first time, I began to see that everything that has come into my life was permitted by God. I began to rejoice in my heart and Spirit, and to thank and praise God as I had never been able to do before. This led me up to that point when I just melted down before God, and with praise and thanksgiving, I asked Him to clean everything out of me that would hinder His working through me. I gave myself up to Him to do what He wants. I no longer want my way. I want His way.

God really honored my prayer. He literally turned my mourning into joy and set my feet to dancing. He also filled me with a peace beyond description, and filled me up with Agape love. To me, it's wonderful. I just can't stop praising Him and thanking Him for all that He has done for me. He really does want us to have joy at all times.

My Comments

Step by step, God permits events in our lives which He knows will help us. If in our ignorance or stubbornness we fail to trust Him, we lose much benefit, and suffer much longer than we need to. If we try to figure out how an event can eventually benefit us, we may be able to think of nothing. But God is not limited to our feeble minds. He can deliver us from the prison of fear.

For my thoughts are not your thoughts, neither are your ways my ways, saith the Lord. For as the heavens are higher than the earth, so are my ways higher than your ways, and my thoughts than your thoughts. (Isa. 55:8-9)

Husband Over-Works

Dear Reverend Carothers,

In my line of work, I frequently run into problems. It's my job to find the solutions. My work is demanding and I've always been very good at it and take pride in my ability to "produce." Unfortunately, my work often requires me to be away from my family at inconvenient times. I've always felt it was my responsibility to "bring home the bacon" and it was my wife's responsibility to run the home and take care of the children. When I would come home from work, I felt I had a right to relax and not have to face problems within the home — after all, I do that all day at work.

I thought my wife was reasonably happy with our marriage, but now she has left, taken our children, and says she is considering divorcing me. Reverend Carothers, there are many women who would be really thankful to have a husband who would provide financially for them as I have for my family. We have a very nice home, live in a good area of

117

town and my wife has never had to want for anything. Yet she claims I've never been a "real" husband and father. As I sit here writing you, I realize that there are ways in which I probably have neglected my family over the years. Yet I've worked hard to provide good things for them. Please pray for God to work a miracle for us. I want my family back. Should I thank the Lord they are gone?

My Answer

Yes, thank the Lord they are gone. Like Martha, you have been busy doing many good things but have left the most important thing undone. You now have the opportunity to take a look and see what has happened.

Your first responsibility was to love your wife as Christ loved the Church. He gave His life for her. He could give no more. You have not given the love your wife wanted and needed. You gave her what you wanted to give. Your children are now suffering from your mistake, but it may not be too late. God has given you this time to see that He also wants your love more than your works. This experience can very easily lead you into a glorious understanding of the grace of God.

If you gave your wife and children your complete love yet failed to supply all their financial needs, they would still be with you and be willing to give their lives to help you. If you give God your love, He will always be there to help you.

Rejoice that your wife is gone. Learn what you can, and believe God will change you and her. Your response to God now can bring you a completely happy life. Center your attention on Christ. Let Him lead you and love your family through you. When you work to earn your daily bread, He will help you to give God what He wants and your family what they really need.

I Know the Reason

Dear Reverend Carothers,

I am presently confined in jail under a charge of armed robbery. I read in some philosophy book once that "to live is to suffer; to survive is to find a meaning in the suffering." I have found that meaning.

I am thirty-two years old, have served time in three different penal institutions, and am an alcoholic. I had tried AA, had read numerous books on Eastern religions, and had even studied Yoga — all without success.

I came to Mississippi the first of this year after being out of prison in Kentucky for eight months. I immediately got involved in starting a drug-rehabilitation program. My ambition was to be of some help to first offenders, to keep them from going to prison by getting them probated to our program. I was very successful in my work, and felt that this was what God wanted me to do. Somehow, however, I started drinking in May, and as a result — my present situation. To say that I was ready to give up would be an understatement. I knew God had a purpose for me, but I couldn't understand why He had to let this happen. I was sorry I had been born.

Then two of your books, along with a handmade cross, were sent to me by a close friend of my mother. As I read *Prison to Praise,* I identified with numerous accounts throughout the book. Previously, I thought I had exhausted every avenue, every possibility of finding a meaning and purpose for my life. But reading your book made me realize that *I am where I am because God loves me.*

What freedom that realization brought to me! It was a real turning point in my life. I am praising God for allowing me to go through, and benefit from, this experience. I am a new person. It's fantastic to think that I had to come to jail in order to be free, but it is true. And I have an inner peace that is beyond anything I had ever experienced before. Praise God and His Son Jesus!

My Answer

I am rejoicing with you that the Holy Spirit has so beautifully shared with you a very eternal truth that God will use all things for our good if we will believe Him. It is hard for many people to understand, but I know that you can find more peace and joy where you are than most people can find on the "outside." Even most Christians expect to find joy in the things that they want. They have not learned to let God take difficult experiences and turn them into pure joy.

I believe that joy will help you win others to Christ. In hundreds of prisons across the United States, men are seeing a real revival. You, too, can be used of God as you give Him your love and careful obedience.

My prayers are with you as you trust in Christ. I will be asking many others to hold you up in prayer.

Wow!

Dear Sir,

All I can say is that you put me on the wildest trip I was ever on. When I decided to practice what you teach about praising God, I stepped into a whole new world. Wow! (or something like that). Is it ever exciting!

My Comments

I wish I could include hundreds of letters that I have received similar to this one. Today is, as one man expressed it, "a whole new ballgame." God is the umpire, as He always has been, but now we know it!

A Sixteen-Year-Old

I am sixteen years old. I am writing to you because I read your book *Prison to Praise*. It really opened my eyes to what's happening with God and the Holy Spirit.

I have been a very jealous person all my life. My girl friend has tried to teach me about God, but it just didn't sink in. I am writing this letter in hopes that you will pray to the Lord for me to become a good Christian. I have sinned so much that it is starting to bother me.

I want Jesus Christ in my life, but I just don't have enough faith. I would like to quit smoking and swearing, but I just can't stop. I have no patience at all. I would like very much to become one of God's children. I would like to receive the Baptism in the Holy Spirit. I go to church on Sundays, but it does me no good to go. It seems I don't get anything out of it. I want God to work through me. I want to become pure inside, with all impurity removed. I feel like an idiot walking around sinning wherever I go. I feel a deep love for God, but I have never had faith in Him. I never thought that He answered *my* prayers, but I know that He will if I become a child of the Lord. Pray for me.

My Answer

Thank you very much for sharing with me the desires of your heart. I am praying with you that Jesus will become very real to you. When you know that He is with you, your heart will be filled with a wonderful joy and a glorious peace.

Please do not keep your attention upon your problem. Your smoking and swearing are only symptoms of what is wrong inside. When you are able to believe that Jesus is living within you, you will then have a great longing to make your life suitable for His presence within you. Until you are able to trust Him to take care of you, it is mighty difficult to give up any bad habits, but when you know that Jesus and His

121

Spirit are working in you, habits often melt away like butter in a hot skillet. I recommend that you read as much of God's word as you can, and especially urge you to get a modern translation of the New Testament. The Holy Spirit will fill your heart with the faith that you want to have in God. Remember, let your mind and your thoughts be filled with what God has written to you. It will not be a big bore, but will become a great joy as you ask the Holy Spirit to lead you.

I recommend that you read several more books that are inspired by the Holy Spirit. *The Cross and Switchblade* and a book called *They Speak With Other Tongues* are two very powerful ones.

I will be much in prayer with you that Jesus will give you His joy and His peace.

My Comments

Many thousands of young people are looking for the real answer. The traditional approach of "go to church on Sunday" will never satisfy the desires of their hearts. The Holy Spirit is moving all over the land and creating a deep desire to know God, and to love Him. This move of the Spirit is reflected in this young boy's letter. Each of us needs to cry out to God that His Spirit will minister through us to meet these very urgent needs. It is becoming clear that even though young people are engrossed in many kinds of harmful activities they want to find a better way. The doors are wide open for you and me to minister to them.

Tragedy?

A ten year old little girl had cancer. The doctor said, "We will have to amputate her arm." Many prayers were offered before the day of the scheduled operation.

One night Jesus spoke to the girl before the operation and said, "You will lose your arm, but you will feel no pain." After the operation, the daughter proudly and confidently announced that Jesus had taken away all the pain. The doctors and nurses could not believe this, and stood by to give a pain-killing shot as soon as one was needed. Hours went by. And days. The child continued to affirm that she had no pain. Until the time of the operation, her reactions to pain had always been normal. She was a living illustration of God's faithfulness to any promise He gives us.

Weeks later, there were signs of cancer all through the little girl's body. Many prayers were prayed by family and friends. Some of them were angry. Her father thought, "If God doesn't heal her, then I don't see how I can ever believe in God."

The child grew worse. She read a book called *Prison to Praise* and started to thank God for her cancer. As her body weakened, she continually thanked God, and her praise gradually transformed her family. The father grew in confidence and trust that God was working in his daughter's life. He fully expected her to rise up and be completely well. But the child's breath weakened, until with one last effort, she said, "Thank You, God," and she was gone.

The funeral was more joyful than a wedding. Hymns of praise and thanksgiving filled the church. God was honored as the giver of every good and perfect gift.

Afterward the father said to me, "As a result of our daughter's sickness and death, we came into the most glorious experiences of our lives. We had never heard of being baptized in the Holy Spirit, but God used our daughter's suffering to bring us to know Jesus in a way we had never known Him. Previously, we had known Jesus as the Savior. We now know Him as a close friend. God used what others might call a tragedy to fill our lives with praise and thanksgiving."

God has now opened doors for this father to be a leader in youth work. His radiant face draws others to Christ in a powerful way. People who know him say, "There has got to be a God who cares, to make this man and his wife like they are."

Yes, God does care, and He permits anything to happen to us that He knows will bless us and others. The real tragedy is that often people permit themselves to be beaten down by the seemingly difficult experiences of life. While they drown in grief and self-pity, the power of God to bring victory goes unclaimed.

I receive at least twenty-five letters a week from husbands and wives who are experiencing what they are convinced is a tragedy. "My husband has gone off with another woman." "My wife has decided she doesn't love me anymore." With great care, they explain how the tragedy has not been their fault, and how wicked and sinful their mate has become. These outcries do not bring them one step closer to victory.

What is the solution? "Affirm God is with me, and He knows exactly what I need. He is permitting this problem in my life because He knows it will help me realize my greatest need. He loves me too much to permit anything to happen that will not in the long run be a great blessing to me."

Is this impossible for you to accept? Then you will have to live in anguish until you become willing to accept it. It is part of God's plan for your life.

This is not to say that He causes marriages to break up. But He uses the problems that develop to strengthen our faith and to force us to depend on Him. Whenever we become so weakened by life that our happiness depends upon another human being, God knows that we need His help. He permits Satan to inflict whatever havoc is necessary to drive us into a position of trust in Him rather than humans. When we have learned what we needed to know, He is able to step in and flood our lives with joy, joy that recognizes Him as the source.

A Diabetic

Dear Mr. Carothers,

Two years ago, when I was eleven, I was put in the hospital with the symptoms of diabetes. I accepted my disease and was a well-controlled diabetic. Last October my Mother really got closer to Jesus. One day she asked me if I thought God could heal me, and I said yes. Then she read Matthew 18:19: "Again I say unto you, that if two of you shall agree on earth as touching any thing that they shall ask, it shall be done for them of my Father which is in heaven." We agreed that God would heal me. And He is doing it. My insulin comes down little by little. Praise the Lord! God let me get diabetes for a reason, and I really do thank Him for it. My life is an adventure, now!

I wrote you this letter because I wanted to tell you I really learned a few things from your book, *Prison to Praise*. I pray for you and I wish you would pray for me, too.

My Comments

Thank the Lord for the faith of a child. We can all learn something from this simple acceptance of God's promise. Candy and ice cream can be pretty important to a teenager, but God will supply every need that is given over to Him. This young girl could already have endured many months of agonizing hunger for candy, but instead, she has enjoyed the peace Jesus offered.

I Thought I Understood

Dear Chaplain Carothers,

I read *Prison to Praise* and *Power in Praise,* and I heard you speaking about praising God for everything. I believed what you said, and praising God for everything had become a firmly fixed part of my life.

Then something happened that tore me apart. I wanted to thank God for it, but couldn't. It was the opposite of everything that I wanted for my life. I could see no possible good ever coming out of the situation. No good at all! The only thing I could say was, "God, I am not able to thank You, but I am willing." I kept telling God this through my tears.

Then the absolutely impossible happened. God took my problem and used it to work out the most glorious peace and joy I have ever had. Life seems so continuously joyful that I've been literally acting like an intoxicated person. The amazing thing is that this new joy keeps going on and on.

My Comments

If God's promises are only for those who live quiet, undisturbed lives, most of us are out of luck. Trouble and strife seem to be shadows that follow us. But God's promises to supply all our needs are as firm and unfailing as the laws of gravity, speed, force, and inertia. Put your faith in God's promise to meet your every need, and God will bring complete peace to you. This is the law He revealed to us through Christ Jesus. Do not be discouraged if you have to go through problems. Personal experience is a far better teacher than anything that others can tell you about God!

Victory in Grief

Dear Chaplain Carothers,

My husband had been an Army chaplain for twenty years when he retired. It looked as if we had many joyful years ahead of us. His death from a heart attack was completely unexpected. I was shattered. I had not prepared myself for anything like that.

But I learned one truth that came to my rescue. I knew that in God's Word I could find help. Each morning I rose at 5:30, went to the beach, and read the Bible. Verse after verse kept telling me to rejoice, be thankful, praise God for everything. Within a few weeks, a marvelous peace filled my heart. As I thanked the Lord for my life as it was, He came to me in a way that was more real than I had ever known before. I knew I was far from alone. How I praise Him for the wonderful power there is in praise. Please keep spreading the message of thanks-giving so many others will know peace instead of grief.

My Comments

One person loses a loved one and endures years of agony. Another steps into the peace that is provided through praise. God provided the mystery of electricity to ease man's burdens. For thousands of years, man did not enjoy this luxury — many still do not — even though provision had been made by the Creator. In the same way, many people still carry their own burdens even though He has provided freedom through praise.

Back Injury

Dear Chaplain Carothers,

First let me apologize for bothering you, but I have a problem that I can't seem to solve. We have a son forty-seven years of age who has been in the U.S. Army since he was eighteen. He had a severe back injury several years ago, and he suffers constantly. He has had surgery three times, has spent some time at Mayo Clinic, and has spent many months in the hospital in his hometown. The Mayo doctors sent him home with a steel brace for his back, and told him they were afraid to attempt any further surgery. He has had to give up all work and activity of any kind.

In your book, Chaplain Carothers, you tell of many miracle healings. I very much believe in God's healing power, but as hard as I pray, I can't seem to get through. My faith has been dampened so many times, in that I have been sick a great deal and have had many financial difficulties.

My only concern now, however, is the illness of our son. He has a wonderful wife and four lovely children, but life is hardly worth living when one suffers with every breath.

I wish I could span the miles and touch your hand in prayer for our son, but since I can't, will you please offer a prayer for his complete recovery? I know that God will hear you.

My Answer

God is also very much interested in the need of your son. Many times a parent does not realize that God is using even sickness to help his children. If you will believe that God is using your son's problem to bless, and to help him, this will release God's power to do what He wants to do. If you are fearful and afraid, you will hold back the healing and saving power of our Heavenly Father. The *natural anxiety* of a mother's love will not release the *supernatural power* of God

128

to bring supernatural healing.

My prayers will be with you as we release our faith together for God to bring help to your son, and joy, and peace into your own life. Remember as you reach out your hand that Jesus is always there to touch you, and to meet your every need. He is praying for you, and knows what is exactly best to meet your situation. Please believe and trust in Him.

Who led thee through that great and terrible wilderness, wherein were fiery serpents, and scorpions and drought, where there was no water . . . that he might humble thee, and that he might prove thee, to do thee good at they latter end. (Deut. 8:15-16)

In Debt

Dear Chaplain Carothers,

I finished reading one of your books last night, *Prison to Praise,* and I want you to pray for me.

I've been a Christian for sixteen years. I was saved when I was twelve years old. I have been terribly depressed since my marriage eight years ago. The relationship between me and my husband is not very pleasant.

The problem is that he can't quit charging things. We're in debt up to our ears. He has a good job and is even a very good personal friend of the governor of our state. We go to church every Sunday. I teach organ, and we both sing in our church choir and teach Sunday school classes, but there is still something wrong.

For eight years, I've lived in prison, you might say, and now since reading your book, I know there's freedom and happiness for me. I know it lies in Jesus.

Please pray for my life and my needs. I feel I can't keep my head up any longer. I praise God for my problem, but I still can't understand why.

My Answer

I am pleased to join you in prayer for your need. It is better that you praise God without understanding why, but I will share with you what I believe is the reason for your problem. If nothing was going wrong in your life, I perceive that you would relax and be so contented, you would not realize your own great need for God.

You find your joy in having the material things in life in good and decent order. If these needs were met, the spirit within you would not be crying out for God's help. Your spiritual need is so great, and God loves you so much, that He permits problems to come to draw you to Himself. If you were out of the human prison you write about, you could still be in a spiritual prison.

I urge you to ask God to baptize you in His Holy Spirit. This may bring you a new set of problems, but you will find great victory in Christ.

In your own church, you may find great disbelief in the power of the Holy Spirit. God will use you to bring new light and understanding to many people, if you will now open your heart and let Him work in your life. He wants to take your depression, fill you with His joy, and then help you to minister to many other people. If you do not know which way to look for help, please begin to inquire about a wonderful group of men called The Full Gospel Business Men. They will be able to give you guidance and will gladly pray for you to be filled with the Holy Spirit. Please let me know if I can help you further.

Why No Tongues

Dear Chaplain Carothers,

You don't know me, but I know the Christ who is in you
will give me the words to write to you because He is my
Christ also. I know He is with me. Although I've been prayed
for with hands being placed on me by devout and dear
Christians, I still do not talk in tongues. What is wrong with
me? Now instead of a joyful spirit, I am walking in a sad and
sorrowful spirit. I desperately want to speak in tongues and
to walk on with my Lord. I believe entirely in the Lord and
know all things are possible. Am I baptized in the Holy Spirit,
or am I only saved? He heals me, hears me, and saves me, but
please, please pray for me. I want more of the Lord's Holy
Spirit. My minister tells me that speaking in tongues is of the
devil.

My Answer

I am praising the Lord that you have not yet been able to
pray in tongues. If you had done so, you would have missed
the opportunity to learn what it really is to pray in the Spirit.
Praying in the Spirit is an opportunity given to us by God to
believe what His Son promised. Turn to the sixteenth chapter
of Mark and find that Jesus gave you a promise. His promise
was to give a new language to everyone who "believed." Your
problem has been not believing what Jesus promised you. If
the Holy Spirit has disregarded your lack of faith, you would
never have realized how important it is to trust in Christ's
promises.

You now realize that when you fail to trust in Jesus, you
do not have a joyful spirit. To disbelieve Christ means to
walk in a sad and sorrowful spirit. This can happen even to
those who have accepted Him as Savior. You can even want
desperately to speak in tongues, but still be bound by your
lack of faith in what Jesus said. You write, "I believe entirely

131

in the Lord and know all things are possible with God," but in this one area you have not believed. Like many people, you believe that He is *able* to give a new language, but you do not believe that He has *already* done it.

Please accept His promise and believe that the new language is yours. If you do now believe, then in faith open your mouth, and let the Holy Spirit speak through you in words that you do not understand. Be prepared for the devil to immediately tell you that it is only your imagination. He tells this to everyone. He always wants to discredit everything that the Holy Spirit does. He wants to cause us to disbelieve everything Christ told us.

You now have the joyful opportunity to decide whether you believe Christ or the devil. Unbelievers may tell you they believe that speaking in tongues is of the devil. Here again you must decide whether you will accept what unbelieving men say or what Christ said. My prayers will be with you.

My Comments

For many years I was uncertain how I should feel toward those who openly said that praying in tongues was of the devil. I tried to keep an open mind so that I would not be critical of those who did not believe as I did. One day the Holy Spirit ministered very powerfully to my heart and said, "You must not remain silent about those who say My work is of the devil."

It became very magnified in my heart what it meant for anyone to accuse the Holy Spirit of speaking by the devil. This was the sin that Jesus spoke out so strongly against. He said that man could speak against God and against Him, but warned strongly against speaking evil of the Holy Spirit. I therefore speak out against any group or organization or fellowship that says speaking in tongues or the Baptism in the Holy Spirit are of the devil. You should have no part of them, give them no encouragement or assistance in whatever they are doing. I do not mean to speak against any organization or body of believers. I am speaking specifically against whatever groups openly condemn the Holy Spirit and

132

declare His working to be of the devil.

There are many who do not yet understand the working of the Holy Spirit, and for them I have only love and understanding. They are praising God and worshiping Him as they understand Him. I am encouraging you to assist them and to love them and to hold them up to God in prayer. He loves them and wants us to love them and their work. People do not have to agree with us in theology and in practice in order for us to have blessed Christian fellowship with them. I am only led to be directly and positively against any person or group who calls the working of the Holy Spirit the working of the devil.

God Changed My In-Laws

Dear Chaplain Carothers,

I have read all three of your books, and I'm going to read *Power in Praise* over again. It was the most difficult of all the books for me to accept. But on looking back, I can recall not yielding myself to a perfect trust in God through Jesus Christ. Although I certainly believe in Jesus, I had become too tense to allow Him to handle my life.

What I really wanted, I think, was a made-to-order Jesus who would jump to my commands and do all I asked, but now I understand what the centurion meant when he told Jesus about being a man of authority, and subject to authority. I have been in the service long enough to know that a good soldier will not question the validity of his commander's actions. He does what he is told, and because he trusts his commander, he trusts that whatever his commander does can be trusted, too. In the same way, I should not order Jesus to do something. I should present my needs before Him and thank Him for them, and because He is my commander, obey and trust Him, thanking Him for everything. There is no joy in questioning the Lord for what He does, but what a joy to put my trust in Him. When I look

133

at my problems, I look to see God working in everything for good, once I have surrendered my problems to Him.

I am interested in more information on how I can help in the Foundation of Praise ministry. I am a Methodist also, and have studied a little about the beginning of the Methodists. This ministry to the souls in prisons and hospitals sounds very much like the ministry of the Wesleys and the early Methodists.

For a long time, I have been praying for my older brother and his wife, and my younger brothers, that they will become Christians. Now I have surrendered them to the Lord for His safekeeping. I know He is taking care of them.

I have been praying with my wife for her parents to accept Christ as their Savior. For quite a while her parents had been nearly at each others throats. Tension was electrical in the air, and my wife was so upset she was in tears as she related the bitterness between her parents. We sat down together and agreed that, because we had been praying for Jesus to touch their lives, God would work some good out of all of it. We thanked God for taking control of the situation, and in five minutes we felt God's Spirit touch us and fill us with such a wonderful glow and peace. We knew God was at work!

The next day my wife went to her parents' house to do some laundry, and when she got home, she said her parents were strangely happy, relaxed, and the atmosphere had completely changed — no more tension, but peace and love. We know that the Lord is beginning a breakthrough into their lives. Every time we see them, they are happier than the last time!

Praise the Lord, Brother Carothers! I praise Him with you! He is the great God. How wonderfully He cares for us all.

My Comments

It is a very beautiful thing to see the childlike simple faith of this serviceman. He has comprehended the beauty there is in turning our problems over to God and trusting Him. In our twentieth century society, we have become accustomed to doing everything for ourselves. We feel compelled to solve

134

every problem and to right every wrong. God, in His mercy, permits us to enter into situations that we cannot change ourselves. In these situations, we learn to turn to God and to trust in Him. When you enter into complicated problems, you need to learn the simple solution of turning them over to God. He will do what you cannot do. Remember that God wants us to have faith in Him.

Throughout the Bible, God looked for men and women who would believe Him. When He found a man who would trust Him, He could accomplish marvelous things. If you desire to be well-pleasing to God, accept the opportunities He has given you to demonstrate your faith in Him. Remember that you were born where you were, and when you were, as part of God's plan for you. He knew, even before you were born, the nature of the problems you would have. He could have stopped your birth, but you were being prepared for His eternal use.

This young soldier knows that no commander wants to have people around who complain and groan over the situation. The commander is aware of what is going on in his unit, and he wants the people under him to trust that he is doing the very best he can in that situation. God, our commander, wants us to believe that through Christ He is working out our lives. The Holy Spirit as the power of God working in this world does not bring His fruit of joy to the heart that is grumbling against God. If you want joy and peace in your life, be thankful and praise God for everything, and the Holy Spirit will do His part.

In thy presence is fulness of joy. (Ps. 16:11)

135

Baby Wouldn't Sleep

Dear Chaplain,

From the day we first brought our daughter home from the hospital, she had never slept more than three or four hours at any one time. She was often awake all night long and fitful all day. She never slept more than eight hours a day from the day she was born and usually only about six hours a day. The doctors could give us no explanation for the tense, upset disposition she had for the first two years of her life.

Then one day I heard you talking on the radio about praising God for everything. I had never heard of such a thing, but I was rocking our daughter as you talked, so I decided to try what you were saying. I thanked God for our baby just as she was. When my mind tried to think of the dozens of sleepless nights and agonizing days she had put us through, I persisted and kept thanking God for her as she twisted and squirmed on my lap. All of a sudden, she relaxed and fell asleep! I put her in her crib and she slept for twelve uninterrupted hours! I could hardly believe it.

That was several weeks ago, and ever since she has slept for twelve hours or more every day. When she is awake, she is as happy as any baby I have ever seen.

Words cannot express how thankful I am to God. I don't understand what happened, but it had to be a miracle.

My Comments

Restless, unhappy people roam all over the world not knowing about the peace Jesus came to bring. This mother touched the source of that peace when she entered into praise, and released God's power to work a miracle.

My Guest Was Late

Dear Chaplain Carothers,

Thank you! Thank you for your book *Prison to Praise.* What a blessing to me personally. The Holy Spirit has truly used it in my life. For the first time, I can praise the Lord for all things without feeling as if I'm lying. I read your book a little over a week ago, and since then, my world has turned upside down as I praise Him for things I'm not happy with as well as for what I am happy with. I can see in such a different light.

By the way, I read your book in about four or five hours while waiting for a friend of mine. We hadn't set a time for her visit, and it was getting late, and I was getting a little angry, thinking she wasn't coming. I thanked the Lord for my anger and for her not coming. Then I realized she wasn't going to come until I finished the book. That's just what happened. We had a wonderful visit. I shared your book with her and thanked the Lord for a whole day.

I could go on and on, but mostly I wanted to share what your book has done for me through the Holy Spirit. There are many things I need to overcome. Now I know I will, because *God's* timing is right.

My Comments

I am often asked how a person can thank the Lord for a sin or weakness in his life.

In order for us to thank the Lord for a sin within us, we must first recognize the sin. It would be impossible to thank Him if we have not recognized it. The Holy Spirit has made us aware of our need so we can be thankful for both the recognition and the sin if we believe God is going to work something good out of it. I know people who flippantly recognize a sin or weakness in their life and carelessly say,

"Praise the Lord." If anyone adopts this careless attitude, he is overlooking a very important part of being thankful to God for all things. The Scripture promises that God will work out all things for good *to those that love God*. Loving God is a very important part of praising Him and being thankful.

If you love a human being and realize that you are doing something that hurts him, what are you going to try to do? Loving someone requires that you do your very best to keep from hurting him. You would therefore leave no stone unturned to find some way to keep from hurting him. If you loved God, you would do everything possible to keep from doing anything that you understand to be wrong. Anything less than doing your best would indicate a lack of love for Him.

We should not permit ourselves to fall into condemnation when we have done the very best that we know how to do. Even for human beings that we love, we can only do what we are able to do. Beyond that, we must trust God and thank Him and praise Him and believe that He will make up for what we cannot do. I am therefore in complete harmony with the verse of Scripture which says, "Whatsoever your hand findeth to do, do it with all of your might." Our Christian living requires that in the midst of our praise, we show our love for our Heavenly Father. Love is never under the bondage of a written law. Love wants to do its best because of the love within and not because of some external requirement.

Greater love hath no man than this, that a man lay down his life for his friends. (John 15:13)

My Mother

Dear Mr. Carothers,

I have a heart filled with thanksgiving for your two books. I will explain why. My mother runs a house of prostitution. For several years I have lived in such shame and self-pity that

I have not wanted to go outside of my home. My husband's work is in this city, and we could not leave. I felt like a prisoner in my home. I was ashamed to go to the grocery store or even to church. I felt so ashamed of my mother. My dear husband kept telling me that it wasn't me, so I shouldn't keep thinking about it. But I couldn't help myself.

I prayed many times for God to deliver me from the horrible burden I felt, but it just wouldn't go away. Then a friend gave me your books. I laughed and cried as I read them. A beautiful peace came into my heart as I realized that God could take even my mother's present occupation and use it to do something good. I really believe that He is going to lead her to Christ. I am very thankful that God is doing something for my mother.

I am now able to go outside of our home with joy and a song inside my heart, for I have stopped thinking of my problem and started thinking of what God is going to do. God has used you to bring a marvelous change into my life. My husband also thanks you, for his life has been changed, as he has a new wife. Everything about our home has been transformed. I no longer sit around feeling sorry for myself. I know that God is truly blessing me with everything good.

My Comments

This letter should give much food for thought to those who have problems of one kind or another with their family. As you realize what God has done for this daughter, perhaps you'll see that He can do marvelous things for you in the situation in which you find yourself. God has promised to use everything for good — if we will trust Him. Satan was using a mother's life to destroy a daughter's peace of mind. Now a daughter is using her praise and faith in God to destroy Satan's work and to draw her mother to Christ.

For this purpose the Son of God was manifested, that he might destroy the works of the devil. (I John 3:8)

A Cab Driver

Peter was angry, bitter, filled with resentment, and he had good reason to be, from a human standpoint. He was in a prison that had a church member as its cornerstone.

When Peter was twenty years old, his parents operated a small bakery in Brooklyn. They worked hard, and by frugal living had put their three boys through high school. A friend in their church had said, "You should expand your bakery so you could hire someone to work for you and not have to work so hard yourselves."

The idea sounded good to Peter and his brothers, so they encouraged their parents to expand the bakery. None of the sons worked in the business, and they wanted their parents to find a way to take it easier in their old age. Further talks with the man in the church revealed that he was willing to lend them the money. They borrowed from him and expanded the business. Everything looked beautiful. The sons rejoiced that their parents would soon be able to relax a little and hire someone to do the hard work.

When Peter's parents made the first payment on the loan, they tried to figure up how long it would take to pay the loan off. They were confused when they discovered that after the first payment, the total amount owed was greater than the amount they had originally borrowed.

"How could this possibly be?" they asked the man who had loaned the money.

"This is what you agreed to on the papers you signed," was his only answer.

They kept making the payments, but the amount owed and the interest due continued to grow. Eventually, the burden became so heavy that they lost the entire business to their fellow church member.

Peter lived with his parents and supported them by driving a taxicab. His bitterness and anger grew year after year. He says, "I laid awake at night thinking up things I could do to

140

that church member who had robbed my parents. The only reason I didn't do anything to him was that I could never think of anything bad enough for what he had done to my parents."

Whenever anyone got into Peter's cab and started any kind of a conversation about religion, Peter would pull to the curb and say, "If you want to get out, okay, but don't talk about religion in my cab."

The parents grew in bitterness as they faced life-long dependence upon their hard-working son.

One day a man left a book on the seat of Peter's cab. He was gone before Peter realized the book had something to do with religion. *Prison,* he read. Then he thought, "That's where that church member would be if there was any justice in this world!"

Because he had nothing better to do, Peter glanced through the first page of *Prison to Praise.* The plot interested him, so he kept reading until another passenger got into the cab. Throughout the day, he read whenever he was free. By late afternoon, he had completed the book and God had reached his heart. All bitterness flowed out with his tears, and he asked God to forgive his own failures.

"God, for ten years I have hated that man. I see now that You have used him to bring me to Christ. Please forgive me and him. Thank You for what he did."

Peace so filled his mind that he yearned to share his new understanding with his mother and father. After dinner that evening, he was sitting in the living room with his father, silently praying for God to show him how to share his discovery with his parents. Just then there was a knock on the door, and his father went to answer it. There stood the man who had robbed them of the business! They hadn't seen him for ten years.

"God has made me so miserable and guilty that I have had to come and beg your forgiveness," he said.

The son's heart leaped for joy. God had already answered his praise. But the father was unmoved and silent.

"Your bakery has grown and prospered. It is worth several

141

times what it was ten years ago. God has told me I must give it all back to you. Here are all the papers you need."

The son could hardly believe his ears. How could God have moved so quickly? When he looked at his father, he knew that a greater miracle had happened. Tears of joy were running down his father's face. The bitterness was gone.

Peter's family is now prosperous, but more importantly, they are a family filled with praise. Yes, the heart of men is deceitful, but God is still able to melt the most stubborn — if we will trust Him.

A Thirteen-Year-Old Speaks

Dear Mr. Carothers,

I am thirteen years old and received the Baptism in the Holy Spirit about two months ago. But I didn't have any joy or peace because I was letting my father depress me. My father is hard of hearing, and he has a bad case of nerves — which makes him talk all the time. I couldn't ever talk to him.

Was I ever blessed when I read *Prison to Praise*. It is the most inspiring book I have ever read. Thanks to you, I'm thanking God for a father like mine. It works! The situation is so much better. I am so grateful. Thank you for the great help you have given me. May God bless you and keep you.

My Comments

I do thank the Lord for the remarkable ease with which children often step into a life of praise and thanksgiving. I urge you to tell children about the wonderful joy there is in praising God for every difficulty. They may be able to assist you in putting into practice what you already believe.

My Husband Died

Dear Chaplain Carothers,

A short time ago I read your books *Prison to Praise* and *Power in Praise*. They have been such a blessing to me, and I felt led to write and share my experience with you.

Last Christmas evening, my husband and the husband of a dear Christian friend were killed in an airplane crash. The accident remains a mystery, humanly speaking, but God in His mercy has given us many indications that this was, indeed, part of His wonderful plan.

My husband loved the Lord with all his heart, and served Him faithfully. His home-going made a strong spiritual impact on many who needed to make decisions for the Lord. We praise Him for this. Our children ages 12, 10, 9, and 6 continually grow stronger in the Lord. Though our loss is great, our blessings and cause for praise far exceed our loss — as long as we keep our eyes on Jesus.

Your books helped me conquer a great battle. My husband had been flying a private plane for some time, and I had always harbored a secret fear of his flying. After the Lord took him, Satan began to cause me to be bitter and to question *why,* especially when I would see or hear a small plane overhead. I would become tense and begin to grieve all over again. I knew this was wrong, and I had to have victory over it.

After reading your books, I began to thank and praise the Lord for the airplane, and for the fact that He chose to use it in the way that He did in our lives. Now, whenever I see a plane fly over, I take it as an opportunity to praise the Lord, and ask Him to continue to use the wonderful testimony that my husband had, through the children and through me.

It does work! Satan's efforts to fill me with bitterness and questions have been defeated through the power of praise.

My Comments

Many people permit the death of a loved one to make them bitter. When this happens, they influence everyone around them. Without wanting to, a parent can cause children to be filled with a resentment against God. The tragedy of doing this is beyond our power to comprehend.

When we lose a loved one, it is essential that we turn our loss over to God and trust and believe that He is working in the situation and that He will bring forth a beautiful plan for the care and guidance of those left behind.

Satan could take your doubt and fear and frustrations and use them to work havoc. Through your faith, God can do many wonderful things.

A Bill Collector Speaks

Good morning,

I'm so happy, I'm giddy. God is truly blessing me and using me in a wonderful way. I feel clean and beautiful inside, all because He loves me.

I gave my employer *Prison to Praise*. He's a faithful church-goer. He told me how much he was enjoying your book but could hardly believe all the miracles taking place in your life. My reply was "Yes, isn't it wonderful!" He knew of the hardships I had been having in the past. I told him how God had blessed me.

This morning he came into my booth to return the book and told me of a miracle that happened to him when he was trying to get into college. His attitude has changed, and he thinks God is using you in a wonderful way. I told him I had *Power in Praise* that he could read and asked if he would like to keep *Prison to Praise* so that his wife could read it. He said, "You may want to give this to someone else," I said,

"Oh, that's all right. I have twenty-four copies in the trunk of my car." The look on his face was startling. Praise God!

I told him I had been witnessing to the debtors. He told me that if I wanted to witness to them to take them into the front booth and take my time with them. Every day has been full of joy for me. Satan jabbed me over the weekend. I obeyed God's voice and restored the peace. I'm going to keep you posted.

Good morning again,

I have to share this with you. Every time I give one of your books away, I'm so overjoyed I could sing — and do. I just seem to bubble over. Right now I want to jump up and down.

This morning I offered to send one of your books to one of my debtors. He refused. However, tomorrow I am to call him again. This afternoon a debtor's grandmother called to plead that I stop attachment against her grandson's wages. I wouldn't budge until she said, "We will have to trust in God." I have just put *Prison to Praise* in the mail to her and another copy to her grandson.

My Comments

Too many people try to keep their faith in Christ outside of their business life. If a business is such that we cannot let Jesus be a part of it, then I believe we are in the wrong business. The writer of this letter has experienced the joy of letting her testimony minister in her everyday life. She took Jesus to work with her. He has promised to honor us as we honor Him. He must abide by His own promise.

Now the Lord saith ... Them that honour me I will honour.
(I Sam. 2:30)

145

A Prisoner Witnesses

My Dear Brother Merlin,

I am in prison, serving a two- to ten-year sentence for dope. I know that God brought me here so I could be freed and find Him through Jesus. I was born again and baptized in the Holy Spirit one year ago here in prison as I read *Prison to Praise.* I have been praising the Lord ever since and working for Jesus, telling everybody the Good News.

The Lord has used me to win two converts so far. One of these has received the Baptism in the Holy Spirit. We are working together in the Lord, to try to bring more convicts to Christ. I think we need a little help from the outside. Can you pray for Jesus' work? We need your prayers.

I just finished reading your book *Power in Praise,* and I really loved it. I know it is true that when you are thankful and praising God for everything that happens to you, He chastens, blesses you, and fills you with joy and happiness and love. I truly thank God and praise Him for bringing me here so that I could find Him.

May God bless you always in your ministry, and fill you with His love.

My Comments

I ask you, the reader, to join with me in prayer for these men and for the many other men who have accepted Christ while in prison. The number is rapidly growing. God is moving by His Holy Spirit to win men in all corners of His world. In your own community, please visit the men in prison, and take them good Spirit-filled books which will teach them about Christ and the power of the Holy Spirit. God has already promised to richly reward you.

*When saw we thee . . . in prison, and came unto thee? And
the King shall answer and say unto them, Verily I say unto
you, Inasmuch as ye have done it unto one of the least of
these my brethren, ye have done it unto me. . . . Come ye
blessed of my Father, inherit the kingdom prepared for you
from the foundation of the world. (Matt. 25:39-40,34)*

A Child Speaks

Dear Chaplain,
   I will be thirteen the 26th of this month. Last night I read
your book *Prison to Praise* and found it really helpful to my
Christian experience. I told God that I would try to praise
Him in all things. When I got to certain parts of your book, I
would stop and praise God that I had a chance to read your
book. Sometimes there would be tears, and I knew God was
trying to tell me something.
   I don't really understand it all completely, but I believe.
   Please excuse the mistakes in this letter, because I don't
know how to type very well.

My Comments

   Often it takes the simple faith of a child to comprehend
the deepest spiritual truth. When we are able to believe
something which we do not understand, we are reaching into
the kind of faith Jesus urged us to have when He encouraged
us to become as a little child. The intellect nearly always
wants to override the Spirit, and it is the intellect that always
gets us into trouble. Our spirit has the potential of coming
into harmony with God's Holy Spirit, and it is to our spirit
that God is now releasing a new day of understanding.

*And it shall come to pass in the last days, saith God, I will
pour out of my Spirit upon all flesh. (Acts 2:17)*

A Beautiful Diamond

Dear Chaplain Carothers,

I read your book *Prison to Praise*. It was beautiful. In some parts I laughed, and in some I cried. I'm writing to you because I need God's help. First, let me explain my life.

I married when I was thirteen, got pregnant one month later, and we separated after about four months. I was going with other boys, even when I was married, and my husband was already married to another woman. I had sex with my cousin when I was only nine years old. After I was married, I had sex with married men and with my husband's uncle. I even had it with children and animals, for which I am terribly ashamed. I went to bed for money — once even with a woman. I stole and smoked dope. At one time, I lived with several men and boys at the same time. Surprisingly, most people didn't seem to know what I was doing. Everyone thought I was just pretty, and a very nice girl.

I know now what a dirty life it was. I caught syphilis. I've taken shots, but it's still in my blood, and I worry about it.

I married again at fourteen, but we were separated after one month, when I found out that he was a homosexual. I still ran around and worked. I married again at twenty-three, and at the same time went out with three other men. My third husband divorced me last year. He is now married again to his fourth wife.

After my divorce I began drinking terribly, cussing all the time, and finally got an ulcer from the way I was living. I was drinking hard liquor so much that the doctor said it would kill me if I did not stop.

I had never been in love with a man, but would live with one for a month or so and then leave him. I stayed with one man, though, for a year, drinking about eighteen cans of beer a day or until I was too tired to drink any more. A few weeks ago, I was put into the hospital because of a bad blood clot in my leg. Just before my trip to the hospital, a man came by my house to talk to people in the apartment about having a Bible study there. I laughed in his face.

When I got back from the hospital, a neighbor gave me a copy of your book *Prison to Praise*. It changed my entire way of thinking, and I began to want God in my life. I telephoned the man who wanted to have a Bible study, and he came to see me. I had a wonderful time hearing about the Bible. Although I had been serving Satan, I had a deep down feeling that I belonged to God. I would not play with Him, because I knew that was wrong.

Thursday, after the first Bible study, I prayed standing by my window. I asked God to remove the devil from me like you had prayed for the woman in your book. I asked Him to let Christ and the Holy Spirit into my body. While I was praying, my feet became numb, as something was being drawn out and up through my body. My chest became heavy, and I could hardly breathe, as something was coming out my throat and almost choking me to death. All the time, I was still praying, and crying. I went blank as I kept repeating, "He has accepted me! God has accepted me!"

I came to myself, crying, and saying, "God has accepted me." I felt so beautiful and happy. But I still have problems. Sometimes I feel that God has not forgiven me. I did so many terrible things. I pray to love God and His children, to really love them. I pray not to hurt anyone with words, or talk about anyone. I pray to love those who do things to hurt me, and to forgive them. I want to love God and have faith and work for Him. I want to be filled with the Holy Spirit and be ever thinking of my Savior and my Heavenly Father.

Chaplain Carothers, I do have so many problems. Please pray for me in Jesus' name. I do believe He will help me. Maybe I don't have enough faith or something. The Lord knows, I don't know what it is. I have begun to thank Him just as you said in your book. I do not question why — I just thank Him.

My Comments

It was my great joy to have the opportunity to pray with this woman in person. It was one of the most thrilling things in my life to see her being filled with the Holy Spirit. When she was baptized in the Spirit, she was literally stricken to the floor. The life that had already been so dramatically changed was now changed even more. Her past life was immediately put to good use. She knew many people who were downtrodden and filled with sin, and she understood them. Her love for people was overwhelming.

Her days were spent in witnessing and telling people what Christ could do for them. There was a magnetism about her testimony that drew people to Christ. The old hardness was gone from her life, and a new radiance could be seen shining all around her. Many people accepted Christ as a result of her testimony, and many are still being drawn to the Lord.

It is easy now to thank God for everything He permitted to happen in her life, in order to take a very crude lump of coal and refine it into a beautiful, shining diamond. God can throughout eternity hold her up as an illustration of what His Son Jesus has done for a human being.

Therefore if any man be in Christ, he is a new creature: old things are passed away; behold, all things are become new. (II Cor. 5:17)

Praise the Lord

Dear Friend in Christ,

Praise God for your books! I have read all three, and they have been a real blessing to me. The Lord has put me in a place where I can find Him and reach Him, and I am very thankful. When my husband left me and our two baby daughters, I had peace over it, even though I didn't praise

150

God for the situation. As I moved along, I could find many reasons why he might want to leave, and I confessed them to God — oh so righteously! After my second daughter was born, I had a real battle with post-partum depression. I never wanted the child, as I had my own ideas of when we should have another child. My husband was very patient all through my pregnancy and stayed by my side even in the delivery room, but I still didn't want the kid.

We were having many financial difficulties and even though we could hardly feed ourselves, my husband was constantly giving to others. Two of them cost us $500. Well, you can imagine the fit this unsurrendered Christian threw!

Our second daughter is a cranky baby, and since I didn't want her anyway, I was cranky right back at her. Her sister was never like that, and I prided myself on having such a good child as she. My husband said our first child was so good because we loved her so much, and our youngest could be too if we would just love her. Me love that! Oh, I would never harm her, and every now and then I mustered up some motherly love. I even prayed that Christ would love her through me. But I didn't love her myself, not really.

Then I read your books. I had gotten my old depression back, and I knew I must do something. The very instant I began reading, I got a blinding headache and tightness in my chest as if all my sins were coming to a head like a boil. I always had a head knowledge that this situation was for good, but never a heart knowledge. So I asked for the Holy Spirit.

The headaches got worse, and I almost choked from the tightness, but I persisted in my will and I spoke in tongues, headache and all. I knew I must call a friend whom I have been jealous of for months because her life seemed so perfect and mine so awful. I did, and we rejoiced in a mutual confession of ill feelings.

Then I realized for the first time that God had to let my husband leave before I could do anything to harm him. I praised God for that in thankful confession. I began thanking Him for everything — even the endless round of dirty diapers. I can't for the life of me figure out their good, but I know in my heart that even dirty diapers have a purpose, so I am thankful.

My husband still isn't home, but I now have peace that soon he will be. I know I can't divorce him as I planned. I must love him with Christ's love and pray for him and ask his forgiveness. I rest assured that this family will be united again in God's good time. Not when my husband has changed, but when I have been changed and thoroughly schooled in walking in the Spirit.

Our baby is still a crab, especially now that she is teething, but to me she's a precious crab, and I really do love her with Christ's love, and that's really all I need. My husband can come home to a wife who praises God for dirty diapers and night-watch and spilled milk and ruined makeup and even vomiting on the freshly shampooed rug.

I still don't really feel overflowing joy at all my tasks, but I am convinced it's because my feelings have ruled me too long. I have glimpses of that joy and am overwhelmed at the prospects. The cloud gets thinner every day. I am convinced that whole and healthy families are in God's will. I am praying for just that and the patience to wait, and the submission to praise Him without looking for a quick result.

The headache and tightness have almost left. Any time I truly seek God, I have a fight with Satan. Won't it be great when he has to stay in hell! Isn't it great that Christ in me has the final victory! Praise the Lord!!

My Comments

This letter is a beautiful commentary on the wonderful power there is in praising God. So very many families are torn apart by the great differences in human personalities. When one or the other party becomes overwhelmed by distress and anxiety, he is almost always cut off from the joy that God wants to give us. This wife has discovered the wonderful reality that no matter what happens, God wants to work something for good in our own lives. The normal reaction is to blame everything on the other person, but she in a very real way has learned to accept the change God

152

wanted to bring about in her own' life. Acceptance has brought her a joy and peace that no kind of rebellion could ever have brought. Her recognition that praising God does not bring instant results in every case has contributed to her faith in God's working out His overall plan. Too often, people try to give a quick try at praising God and then flee back to self-pity when they think it hasn't worked.

This wife has realized that often God permits a separation or even a divorce to save one of His children from destruction. The distressed mate may, by indulging in over-possessive love, be refusing to permit God to take care of the ones that *He* loves. If we truly love someone, we must then be willing for God to work out his life in whatever way He knows is best. If we tenaciously cling to the statement, "But the Bible says," we may overlook many other things which the Bible says. It is possible to cling to one phrase of Scripture and overlook many other passages which direct us to trust God and believe that He is working out something for our own lives, and for others, even though we do not understand it. We are not called upon to understand, but to believe.

From a Priest

I want to thank you for the inspiration I found in reading your book, *Prison to Praise.* I read it all today and I am looking forward to reading *Power in Praise.* I am uncertain about many things in myself, and I am really looking, but I believe I'm often misled and end up in a dead end. I know God loves me, but I am often discontent with myself and have a poor self-image. I feel resentful toward my peers – jealous, afraid, up-tight – and always seem to be running away from myself. I put up a front many times of being other than I am, and have a real battle with thoughts and imaginations.

I was prayed over for the Baptism in the Spirit a while

153

back by some Catholic Pentecostals, but I still bear these mixed-up feelings and really freeze. I'm afraid to open up.

Your faith seems so strong that I'm encouraged to ask you to pray for me for a healing in these matters. I have a few hang-ups with impure thoughts and desires; I am fearful of my feelings, and fearful that I'm not doing the Lord's work — feeling compelled to fail. At times I even doubt my calling. I just don't feel my heart is in my life. Perhaps the devil is trying to trick me into looking too much for natural fulfillment. I need balance.

I know I should praise God right now for my life, as confused as it is. (I just did.) I've been ordained many years and feel it's time for another conversion of heart. I need to be pushed in the right direction and keep on going steadily. I'm always afraid of souring the situations I am in. I think basically I'm afraid of women (with all my imaginings), somewhat closed to men (unhappy and unwilling to share), and I don't have enough discipline in my life.

Can your faith help me? I just seem afraid to live — the opposite of you — although you do share (rather you *did* share) my feelings about getting up in the morning.

I really want to get Jesus across to people. I need His Spirit, but I feel chained down to my self and sometimes become overly clerical and businesslike (dead is the word). Like Lazarus in the tomb, I stink! Praise the Lord, He can raise me up. Please pray for a brother in need so that he can be numbered among those who have felt God's power working through him.

My Comments

I have omitted from this letter details which would indicate the name of this my brother in Christ. I have included this letter to help you to see that problems are not limited to those who earn their living in the secular world. I also want you to recognize the great need there is to not criticize a member of the clergy who seems to be like Lazarus in the tomb. Men who recognize a deep spiritual need often do not know what to do about it. They should not be

154

criticized, but loved, regardless of how cold or how spiritual a minister may seem to be. Do not take for granted that his heart is satisfied to remain where it is.

This letter indicates the deep cry that is often in the heart of a pastor as he longs to be of greater help to his people. Your love for him could be the very thing that would lift him into a new dimension of praise. His potential for leading others to Christ may be much greater than your own, but God could use your love and kindness toward him to set him free from bondage. I do not mean that you are compelled to remain under the ministry of a man who is not building your spiritual life, but you can, as the Spirit leads you, minister to those whom God has brought into your life. You can go out of your way to express your love and concern for them even when they do not seem to respond.

I am continuing to remember in prayer the priest who wrote this letter. I invite you to join me in prayer for him. One day we will hear that God has filled his heart with the joy he so earnestly longs for.

Now unto him who is able to do exceeding abundantly above all that we ask or think, according to the power that worketh in us, Unto him be glory in the church by Christ Jesus throughout all ages, world without end. Amen. (Eph. 3:20)

In The Will of God

Dear Chaplain Carothers,

I just want to thank you for your three books. They have helped me so much, through so many trials, especially when other Christians would act as if these terrible things were happening to me because I was out of the will of God. I would feel so discouraged and feel as though I had no faith at all. Then I would read your books and begin praising God and feel the joy of the Lord return.

Lately our prayer groups have had some teaching on binding Satan every time you meet, binding him all the time even out of our own minds — and every time I would get involved in these teachings, I would feel that fear start coming back. When I know God has control of every area of my life, and I praise Him, my fears disappear. He is faithful and He will see me through.

My Comments

The growing recognition of what Satan is able to do is causing many people to fix their attention on Satan himself. Your attention is fixed on the person you are following, and we are told in the Scriptures to follow Jesus. He is leading you out of where you have been and into a new place. He does not want your attention on the past but rather on His future for you. If you know you are in the wrong place, it will do you no good to fix your attention on the one who has led you to the wrong place. He will lead you into even worse places, regardless of what you do. Jesus is your only hope for peace, joy, and God's grace.

Conclusion

Whatever your position may be, you must realize that for evil to exist, an almighty God would have to permit its existence. Once you realize this, you will probably ask, "Why does He permit it?" The only logical answer for a perfect, loving God would be, "He intends to use evil to accomplish something good."

You may know of several evil events in your life that have eventually resulted in something good. If there are some evils that you have seen no good in, surely you know that all knowledge and wisdom are not yours. God has promised to work everything for our good if we trust Him. Isn't it reasonable for Him to ask you to trust Him? If God permits evil in your life, it could only be to help you or someone else.

Matthew tells of Jesus being driven into the wilderness to be tempted of the devil. Have you thought of what drove Jesus? It was the Spirit! The Holy Spirit drove Jesus to a situation where He could be tempted by God's enemy. This was God's plan for Jesus. He had to endure temptation. Jesus urges you to rejoice when you are tempted. He knew that no evil power could force its way into your life unless God permitted it. And why should God permit it? For His own perfect reason. We are far too human to understand all His plans, but we do have the right to trust Him.

James, writing by the inspiration of the Holy Spirit said, *"Brethren, count it all joy when ye fall into divers temptations; Knowing this, that the trying of your faith worketh patience. But let patience have her perfect work, that ye may be perfect and entire, wanting nothing!" (James 1:2-4).*

Revelation tells us that even after Satan has been bound for a thousand years, God will again release Him. This makes it crystal clear that God has complete authority to do His own will in His own time. Since His will is dedicated to working out everything for the good of His children, I have determined with my will to trust Him. You have the same right, and with this determination to trust God comes a release of the same power that was in Jesus. The mighty power of the Holy Spirit manifests Himself in everyone who will believe and trust and praise the Father. Freedom is yours through praise!

The neglect of a truth, followed by its rediscovery, often results in extreme overemphasis that can be very detrimental to spreading of the truth. If any truth is exaggerated, it gets out of proportion. Because of my exuberance and special interest in praise, is it possible that I may be overemphasizing its importance? Some would say yes. If I listen to them, I will change my ministry. If I look at Scripture, what will I do?

There is a superabundance of Scriptures regarding praise, thanksgiving, and rejoicing. Most of them have to do with the amount of time, energy, and thought we are to devote to praising God and thanking Him. "In every thing give thanks" (I Thess. 5:18). This indicates there will be "things" in our lives and in these "things" we are to be giving thanks. This does not shut us off from the rest of the world or make hermits out of us. We are in "things" and in "thanks" at the same time. We are involved with life as it is for us and involved in giving thanks at the same time. Things without thanks can become so burdensome that life becomes barely worth living. Thanks without "things" could so separate us from the world as it is that we couldn't minister Christ to those who need Him most. Put the two together, and you will have a powerful force that will give you continual overflowing joy in the midst of the most difficult circumstances. And you will be kept in regular contact with the average man and woman who desperately needs to hear about Jesus.

Men need not only to hear about Jesus but to hear about Him from someone in whom they can have confidence. Our learning to live in the world as it is and still be completely at peace is a testimony to them that if you can do it, they may be able to do it, too! If you, in complete peace of mind, say, "I received this through Jesus," they will tend to respond with, "If He did this for you, perhaps He will do it for me, too!"

158

And you know He can and will. Or do you? If life is a series of ups and downs for you, you cannot say to others "Christ gives me the complete victory He promised." (Or at least you cannot say it and be truthful.) People do not listen very much to what any of us say. They are too accustomed to being bombarded with all kinds of propaganda about toothpaste and soap to swallow anything without seeing it work.

If you say, "Jesus really is the answer to all of life's problems," they will want to observe His being the answer to all of your problems. If they see that He is, they will still wonder, "Can He be my answer, too?" But if they see He does not give you what they would like to find, they will probably let your words flow in one ear and out the other. Self-survival has taught modern man to do just that.

The disciples not only said, "Jesus is the answer," they demonstrated that He was the answer for their own lives. Have you heard churchgoers grumble and complain about one thing and another? Their complaints are probably justified from the natural viewpoint. But where is their victory in Christ? His victory is supposed to be *in everything*. *Everything* does not leave loopholes for odds and ends not to be included!

When Paul ended up in prison, after having been beaten, he was securely chained to the prison floor and as an extra precaution, placed in the part of the prison that was below the ground. His reputation for "victory" had preceded him. People had learned about the power that rested in Paul because of his allegiance to the One called Jesus Christ. In this prison cell, Paul demonstrated the victory in Christ he had preached. He did not snap the chains with the strength of Samson. He did not grumble that God gave Samson great physical strength and him none. Nor did he grumble because the three Hebrew children went into the fiery furnace and came out unhurt. His hands hurt from the pain of the chains. His back ached from the leather whips that had been used on him. But — because he knew God was working out His perfect plan for his life — whatever God wanted was what Paul wanted. He did not just accept his weakness as

159

something he could not do anything about. He rejoiced that he was exactly as God wanted him to be. He rejoiced that he was exactly *where* God wanted him to be.

In the midst of Paul's singing and rejoicing, God stepped in to change Paul's situation. Paul had learned the lesson God wanted him to share with us. *"Rejoice in the Lord always: and again I say, Rejoice."* (Phil. 4:4). Rejoice where you are and in whatever state you are, because you know you are victorious in Christ.

When the prison keeper saw what happened in Paul's life, he wanted the same Jesus in his life. When people see your victory, they will want your Jesus. You may long for the opportunity to preach Christ before a multitude of men. God wants you to preach Christ where you are and to whomever you contact. You may not need to say one word; *but you need to be in complete victory in Christ.*

Complete victory and grumbling do not go together. On election night, the victorious candidate does not grumble about the people who failed to support him. He heaps volumes of praise on those who did support him. The time for rejoicing is at hand. In the camp of the defeated, they grumble over failures, lack of support, and try to determine what they have done wrong.

Which candidate do you support? If Jesus is your sponsor, and you sponsor Him, do you know that He has already been victorious? God has declared Him the victor. He came to the world and endured every temptation that Satan could fling at Him. He came through perfect, without spot or blemish. On the cross He provided our victory over even grief and sorrow: "Surely he hath borne our griefs and carried our sorrows" (Isa. 53.4). If we declare Him to be victorious and then go around with grief or sorrow, the people who see us will naturally think, "If He is 'victorious' like *they* are, then He certainly can't do anything for me." Once again, through our lives, "we did esteem him smitten of God, and afflicted" (Isa. 53:4). Our lives made Him seem defeated.

If we as Christians have the mistaken idea that followers of Jesus are never to have trouble, I'm pleased that the majority of non-Christians do not have that idea. They do

160

not look for examples of men who have no problems. They do look for men who have problems similar to theirs, yet live in joy and peace. The testimony of a man who knows what it is like to suffer means something to a man who is suffering and wants to find answers.

The Communists tell people, "Listen to us and we will take away all your problems and give you ease and luxury the rest of your lives." As soon as the Communists are in power, they give men burdens ten times greater than they had before. The capitalist says, "I will give you nothing; but I will show you a way to work whereby you can receive everything you need." This perhaps is not the quick easy solution, but it is the one that works.

Jesus did not come to "take us out of the world" but to give us victory *in* the world. His peace is a peace of the heart. He meets a man where He is and fills him with rivers of living water that flow from within. As a man receives this inner living water, he does grow in strength to the point where he can control even the natural environment in which he lives — but this comes as he loses fear of the world he lives in. Remember Peter's experience on the water? For a brief moment, he was able to believe that Jesus supplied everything he needed, and he walked on top of the water. Then he was afraid. The result? He sank.

Fear that maybe Christ is not victorious in your situation will cause you to sink. People will say, "He is sinking like I am. Why should I follow his God?"

You may not be called by God to walk on the water; but He has called you into your present situation. Believe that He is in it with you, supplying all your need, your complete victory, and He will manifest Himself in you. Others will be amazed that you are living in peace and they will be drawn to your source.

Publishers note:

Comments, inquiries, and requests for speaking engagements should be directed to:

Merlin Carothers
Box 2085
Escondido, CA   92025